The
EMPLOYEE
Experience

The
EMPLOYEE
Experience

A Capstone Guide to Peak Performance

JANE MCLEOD, RN, MSN • **SUE TETZLAFF**, RN, RHIA, MHA, FACHE

Foreword by Michael Henry Cohen

NORTHLOOP
BOOKS

NORTHLOOP
BOOKS

North Loop Books
322 First Avenue N, 5th floor
Minneapolis, MN 55401
612.455.2294
www.NorthLoopBooks.com

ISBN-13: 978-1-63505-115-5
LCCN: 2016902667

Distributed by Itasca Books

James Arneson, Cover Designer
Anna Kiryanova, Typesetter
Neal McLeod, Content Editor
Andrea Eves, Art Director
Korinne Lamoreaux, Photographer

Printed in the United States of America

and ever-changing world. I recommend *The Employee Experience* to those ready to assess and augment their leadership tool box. You will not be disappointed."

— Terri Potter, Potter Consulting, Former President/
CEO Meriter Health Services

"This book is a treasure box of ideas and strategies to engage my team that are genuine, practical and smart. As an experienced nurse leader, I thought I knew all I had to know about engaging my wonderful staff. I was wrong! I found myself humbled from the first chapter on Purposeful Rounding and this continued throughout the book. I discovered there is still so much to learn and so many ideas to try."

— Rita Jury, Nurse Administrator

"Jane and Sue have created a leadership reference book that produces results — their focus on employees and how to build relationships in the midst of the daily 'whirlwind' is brilliant. The solutions format for the chapters make the information accessible as situations arise along your leadership journey; the book provides realistic, easily implemented tools that any leader can use to improve outcomes in their work environment."

— Marialena Murphy, Nurse Leader,
Author, and Teacher

"Wow! *The Employee Experience* is amazing. It's all there; with a commitment by the leadership team, hard work and lots of energy, you have written the plan for organizational success and an amazing employer to work for! I loved attending your leadership summits but having this reference to refresh the learning is a tremendous asset to continue the learning experience. One of the best leadership books I have read!"

—Carol Stoll, Retired Chief Nursing Officer,
Covenant Healthcare

Contents

Who are Sue Tetzlaff and Jane McLeod? A snapshot of leadership capability and a how-to guide on using this book as a resource for your leadership.

by Jane McLeod

This Solution teaches leaders how to really and truly create employee engagement in their work environments through relationship building.

by Sue Tetzlaff

This Solution focuses on mustering the will and mastering the skill of leadership conversations that lead to peak performance.

by Jane McLeod

The power of positivity in your leadership gets a real shot in the arm. Recognize some things about yourself and your effect on others in this Solution.

This Solution guides leaders to put a stop the hiring madness! Turn around the practice of "hiring for skill and firing for behavior." Instead, hire for behavior and train to skill.

This Solution gives leaders a new perspective on the diversity of their team. How does a millennial like to be communicated with? The answers to why your team may not be functioning to its best ability may lie in this Solution.

This Solution invites leaders to adopt a new structure for change management and twenty-first-century leadership through the empowerment of employee-driven teams.

This Solution challenges leaders to elevate the trust factor in their team and organization through transparent communication. You'll love the one-on-one communication and organization-wide strategies for conveying your most important messages.

Improvement is continual. Peak performance requires persistence. Those leadership efforts that seem to fade or lose excitement can come alive again for you and your team.

Foreword

While engaged in a career specializing in team development and employee relations, I have had the privilege of working with a variety of truly outstanding leaders. Each leader has his or her own unique management style, yet all share some common characteristics. Successful leaders:

- Serve as role models for the attitudes and behaviors expected of others. They lead by example.

- Operate from quiet strength. They are comfortable in their own skin and don't feel the need to flaunt their power or demean people.

- Display genuine passion about their work, and their enthusiasm is contagious.

- Demonstrate sensitivity to employees' psycho-social needs. Their primary focus, however, is on achieving high-quality results. They believe that happiness on the job is largely a byproduct of success.

▓ Enjoy recognizing achievement while always looking for opportunities to improve performance.

▓ Take the time to understand the history and culture of their work group before making significant changes. Whenever appropriate, they include employees in decision-making processes on issues that directly impact their work. They partner with employees, utilizing them as internal consultants.

▓ Communicate a common vision that transcends individual self-interests, cultural, and work-style differences and hold people accountable for outstanding outcomes.

Successful leaders understand that the alternative to establishing a culture of employee engagement and accountability is to accept marginal performance, a litany of excuses, and a plethora of unhappy people who feel immune from the consequences of their actions. And without a common vision that unites people, employee unity splits into disparate parts; different factions form as personal agendas get served and pettiness thrives.

The *Employee Experience* is important reading because it outlines in practical terms how to tap into the collective wisdom of employees in order to achieve outstanding results. It provides easy steps to implement engagement strategies that will result in attaining employee commitment to the team's mission, vision, and values. It helps the leader anticipate, plan for, and overcome resistance to change.

The exercises and illustrations in this book are grounded in reality. They have been tested on the ground and have been proven to be effective. Properly applied, they can make a profound difference in the quality of customer and employee relations.

— Michael Henry Cohen

Michael Henry Cohen is the president of Canoe Press and Consulting Services and is the author of *The Power of Self-Management, What You Accept Is What You Teach, Time to Lead,* and *The Power of Shared Vision.*

Introduction

We want businesses to be great. Customers deserve it. Employees deserve it. We bet you want your organization, in whatever industry you are in, to be great, too. Though greatness can seem elusive, we have experienced time and time again that mediocrity can be replaced by greatness. This journey starts with a commitment to creating an amazing Employee Experience, which leads your organization to Peak Performance. How do we know this? We have taken that journey.

While the vast majority of our experiences and the stories we share within this book come from our time in healthcare, we don't believe that great leadership is mutually exclusive to any particular industry. Great leaders can be found in small teams that inhabit rooms in the deepest of sublevel basements, to massive, multifaceted conglomerates that operate on a global scale. Inspiration, motivation, dedication—these are attributes that belong to human beings, not buildings or LLCs. Similarly, we uphold that the solutions contained within these chapters are just as applicable to non-healthcare organizations.

We've created *The Employee Experience* as a go-to resource designed to equip and inspire others toward positive change. This book is focused on people: people's behavior, performance, and contributions to the organization. As we've learned, in order to create great results, you first need to create a great employee experience.

Given that this book is coauthored, you will notice two "voices" or writing styles alternating between the twelve Solutions, or chapters. The vision for creating this book in this way was born out of several years of co-teaching public training sessions. The positive feedback from our audience members speaks to the appreciation of two different and distinct leaders who complement each other well.

Our styles may be different, but our passion for improving work environments and organizations is the same. Jane, whose diverse professional background spans from the bedside of patients to many levels and roles of leadership, is often described as someone who is positive, easy to relate to, witty, and well-grounded. Sue, who has spent nearly all of her career serving in various senior leadership roles, could easily be labeled as an overthinker and geeklike and often illogically optimistic.

Below is the story of how our professional lives intertwined during what we refer to as "a journey to peak performance."

A Journey to Peak Performance

For two decades we worked together as part of a team, leading healthcare in our community. In our rural and isolated community in northern Michigan, our community's hospital is the main access point for healthcare. Yet, as important as this one-hundred-year-old asset is, it has experienced great challenges that could have led to the loss of its value, or its existence.

It was 2005 when we sat with our peers, the senior leadership team of our community's hospital, digesting report after report and one graph after another that collectively painted a dismal picture of our organization. If the operational metric should be going up, it was trending down. If the metric should be going down, it was trending up.

In the face of this extreme challenge, we were determined to not lose this asset for our community. We knew this was going to take more than a small tweak to our existing strategic plan. In response, we assembled a fourteen-member steering team of physicians and leaders. We dug deeper into further study of our situation. We read and we researched. We were detectives searching to discover what made a hospital, or any business, great. We wrote plans. We wrote white papers. We met for hours each week to discuss and debate solutions. Incredibly, we did this for two years. Not surprisingly, we learned a lot. Unfortunately, over those two years, our ugly picture got uglier. The organization slipped deeper into trouble.

As the story unfolds, in 2007, after two years of research and in the face of an uglier picture, we started to act on all that we had learned. Our first bold step was to place the overly researched and debated plans and solutions into the hands of employee-populated teams. One key strategy was to move away from the mind-set that the fulfillment of the organization's mission, vision, and strategic plan was only the work of leaders. It was the work of everyone in the organization.

As leaders on this steering team, we guided and empowered the employees on these teams to act on plans and solutions to heal our broken hospital. We learned along the way that some of the plans needed adjustment, so those got revised. We discovered that some of the solutions didn't work at all, so those got dropped, and we moved on to the next one. Fortunately, our efforts led to amazing results. The organization was bigger and stronger than it had ever been in its lengthy history. Its value to the community multiplied.

As we worked together orchestrating transformational change in our community hospital, we had a vision for where those efforts would take our organization. Yet we hadn't contemplated where this journey would take us personally or professionally. That it would lead us beyond the boundaries of our own community to dedicate ourselves to inspiring positive change in healthcare and leadership all across the country was something we didn't foresee.

What started out as our professional responsibility to the hospital that employed us evolved into an opportunity to assist other leaders and organizations through leadership training offerings and partnerships over the past several years. This led to organizing the key components of our organization's transformation into three parts: Framework, Structure, and Solutions. It also called upon us to apply these components to other organizations to assess if the results were replicable.

We now know that organizations can garner big and fast results with the successful adoption of a Framework, Structure, and Solutions. Take, for instance, the changes in these healthcare organizations:

- A hospital in Wisconsin that within one year improved employee engagement from the thirty-eighth percentile to the seventy-ninth percentile and moved the inpatient and emergency room patient satisfaction into the top five to ten percentile of the nation.

- A hospital in Michigan that within eighteen months moved to the number-one ranking in the state for inpatient satisfaction as measured by the nationally standardized patient survey. A year later, at the time of this writing, they remain at the number one rank. While at the top patient satisfaction rating, they have also achieved 100 percent compliance with all publicly reportable inpatient quality standards.

Through working with organizations such as these, we are affirmed in our belief that the Employee Experience is the driving force behind these great results. But you can't get to greatness alone. If organizations ask for our help to improve their quality, safety, finances, or customer satisfaction, we can only be successful if they commit to transforming their Employee Experience.

Yet how do we do it? The odds aren't in our favor. It is estimated that 70 percent of transformational efforts fail. There is no magic. There is no pixie dust. There is, however, an amazing collection of research and knowledge regarding what works. Positive change is about putting it together and putting it in place.

Our "putting it together" approach is defined as the Framework for Achieving Great Results (see Appendix 1). The Framework, initiated in our community hospital's turnaround, has evolved over the years as we have learned more from applying it in other organizations.

Our "putting it in place" approach is the assembly of employee-engaged teams into a Structure. This Structure (see Appendix 2) is the "hierarchy outside the hierarchy." This is in keeping with decades of research on leadership and change by John P. Kotter that led to his recommendation of creating "dual operating systems." One operating system, the typical management-driven hierarchy, has the purpose of managing the current day-to-day operations while the employee-driven operating system gets to work at innovation, transformation, and culture development. And the key to the structure of this second operating system is that it is employee, not leadership, driven.

To complement the Framework and Structure are a series of Solutions. These Solutions are the evidence-based practices, best practices, and high-performance work practices that we have uncovered along the way. Inside and outside of your organization, there is greatness. In all types of organizations there are individuals, teams, or departments that are doing amazing things. They are working within the same constraints and resources as everyone else, yet prevailing at being great.

This book is a forum for us to get these Solutions related to improving the Employee Experience into your hands. It is designed with individual leaders, teams of leaders, teams of employees, and entire organizations and systems in mind. Everyone, individually or collectively, can make a positive impact on the employee experience. And when you do, you will see those ripple effects in positive results in other aspects of operations, such as financial results and growth.

Now you may be thinking that you aren't in a leadership position that would make it possible for you to champion an organization-wide transformation. Maybe you were just looking for a few tips to elevate your leadership. Or maybe you are a new leader, and you just want to know where to start. This book has lots to offer you.

To achieve greatness, we have to proactively invest time in activities that move us closer to goal attainment. Reading this book and approaching the Call to Action at the end of each Solution with diligence will be an investment of time. When we proactively invest the time that improves the future state of our leadership, our work unit, our organization, the day-to-day reactive commotion (which we refer to as the "whirlwind") calms down and achievements go up.

This book is in your hands as a sign of your willingness to invest. For whatever reason, you are at the point of reading a book on improving the employee experience. We wish you much success as you move forward with the information contained within these pages.

Some suggested ways to approach this book as a resource for your leadership include:

1. Read it through, take what you need, and put it into action.

2. Read it through, then prioritize the Solutions into a customized improvement plan. Take the time to triage the Solutions to prioritize the implementation of those that will benefit your leadership and your work unit the most.

3. Or, develop your own creative way to use this resource and the Solutions it contains.

What we know is that you likely can't successfully implement all Solutions at once. Change is hard. And behavior change is the hardest. Many of these Solutions will require behavior change.

As with any improvement effort, we should narrow the focus. Consider one or, at most, a few Solutions that may assist in your efforts to improve the Employee Experience. Then, just start. And when you are ready for more, move on to adopting another Solution or two.

Customize these Solutions to make them yours (or make them better) and soon your employees will be saying what an amazing place they work for.

If you are a team of leaders in an organization, approach number two above can also be used to create a plan to implement the Solutions within the entire organization. This creates a system of standardized leadership that promotes synergy and a further-reaching culture change and transformation.

If you are a member of an Employee Experience Team by whatever name you call yourselves, approach number two will also help you to prioritize the Solutions that are right for your team and organization.

While prioritizing Solutions for adoption, be mindful that this is not a "flavor-of-the-month" approach. Stay the course and keep improving the aspects of the Solutions. This is where Solution Twelve — Review, Readjust, Refresh, Reconnect, and Re-Inspire — comes into play. After assessing, planning, and executing a Solution, be diligent in following through with evaluating and adjusting. Over time, the more you evaluate and adjust, the more results you will gain from a Solution. This successful approach is adapted from the commonly used continual improvement model of Plan-Do-Study-Adjust (PDSA).

We also advise that you not take the Solutions as overly prescriptive. We challenge leaders, employees, and organizations to find a way to "one-up" an already great idea or practice. We encourage a method publicized as the CASE (Copy and Steal Everything) method. And we've expanded the advice to: Copy and Steal Everything, but make it yours and make it better!

Our Capstone mantra is "Just Start." As our community hospital transformation journey taught us, you don't have to have it all figured out to move forward. And as Zig Ziglar says, "You don't have to be great to start, but you have to start to be great."

We wish you well on your journey to greatness — a journey focused on creating an amazing Employee Experience, which leads your organization to Peak Performance.

Purposeful Rounding

Leadership is not about titles,

positions, or flowcharts.

It is about one life influencing another.

—John Maxwell

Relationships, relationships, relationships. This is the mantra all leaders need to live by. Relationships bind an organization together. They gather all the tremendous talent held under one roof under a single banner. They give higher purpose to the work that is to be done.

The entire premise of this book is built on the overriding principle that when you lead effectively in order to engage your employees to behave, perform, and contribute at a higher level, good things happen. Your platter of leadership tasks gets smaller because your employees want to assist in the leadership of their work environment. Your results begin to improve. Your strategy comes alive because you have communicated it well, and others believe in it and want to work for an organization that keeps track and is winning.

Developing a relationship with the people who work with you and for you is where it all starts. As a leader, you cannot lead your people on to the battlefield that is your department or organization every day without knowing their "why." What motivates them to come to work? What makes them tick?

Recognizing and becoming familiar with these employee attributes is a key driver to engagement. Rounding is a very simple, effective tool to use to get you there. While effective, it doesn't happen overnight, meaning, you will not see the results instantly the first day you round. This is not comfort food for the leader's soul. This is amazing shoot-you-over-the-moon-with-success stuff. Yet it takes a consistent investment of your time each day you work, and that requires your commitment.

Then suddenly, after a period of weeks, you will come to work one day and not be hit with the latest whirlwind. An employee will have taken care of the whirlwind for you. Employees will be performing, behaving, and contributing at a higher level. Those who are not will be very obvious to you. Fear not! We have a chapter that outlines how to deal with those situations.

This solution outlines the "why" of rounding daily in your leadership life. It needs to be more than exercise and flossing of your teeth. It needs to be the oxygen you breathe. You cannot survive without it. Within this solution, I also describe the "how" of rounding with tips to make it easy for you to integrate rounding into your daily work.

Your role as a leader is to create a work environment where happy, productive, and loyal people can flourish. (Note how I did not say you have to *make* them happy!) Two things that can prevent you from making this happen are a *lack of information* and a *lack of time*. You can avoid the lack of information by *rounding with purpose,* and you can avoid the lack of time by *decreasing the whirlwind* with purposeful, systematic rounding.

What Is Purposeful Employee Rounding?

Employee rounding is dedicated time that leaders take to talk (usually one-on-one but could be in a small group) with employees. It is a relationship-building conversation versus simply conveying information or a quick hello.

Tom Peters and Robert Waterman in their 1982 landmark book *In Search of Excellence* coined the phrase "management by walking around." As our world becomes more connected via emails and texts, leaders could easily choose to stay in their offices. The Hewlett-Packard executives ran their company outside of their offices after Mr. Peters and Mr. Waterman published their book. The basic premise is that leaders should never manage their departments by email. A physical presence is often required to really know what is going on in the day-to-day operations and relationship building crosses the boundaries of all leaders in any industry.

Rounding takes "management by wandering around" or "leader visibility" to a new level. The format of rounding leads to purposeful, systematic conversations that focus on positives as well as important aspects of work.

While rounding, you are finding out *proactively* how to lead. When you round daily and are very purposeful and systematic in the questions you ask, you will gather information to act on or to delegate. When you do this, the reactive commotion we refer to as the whirlwind slows down around you. Issues will be addressed at the lowest possible level.

4

Sample Employee Rounding Questions

General

1. How are you?

2. What is going well today?

3. Tell me something about yourself that I didn't already know.

4. Name something positive happening at work today.

5. Are you aware of anything that may pose a safety risk to our customers, employees, or visitors?

6. Is there any equipment broken or missing?

7. What equipment or supplies would help you do a better job?

8. Do you have the tools and equipment to do your job?

9. What training could we offer that would assist you in carrying out your job?

10. What educational pursuits do you have?

11. Do you have your next job in mind?

12. Is there anything I can be doing differently to support you?

13. What opportunities do you see for me to improve my leadership?

14. I want to always be improving my leadership. Can you tell me one thing I could do differently?

15. Is there something going on in the organization that you don't fully understand or would like to know more about?

16. Is there anything else I should know or any questions I can answer for you?

17. Who may I thank for doing a great job?

18. Tell me about a coworker who has done something you would define as excellent.

Healthcare

1. What keeps you awake at night regarding patient safety?

2. What is one way we can improve patient safety?

3. Do you have a desire to achieve certification?

4. How are you finding the new *medication reconciliation* process to be working?

5. What outcomes are you seeing with the implementation of *hourly patient rounding*?

6. What employee, physician, or department has gone above and beyond to serve a patient well?

6   The Benefits of Employee Rounding

For more than a decade, rounding was a practice that was central to my leadership. It aided in creating an amazing employee experience, which led to the achievement of amazing operational results. The multitude of benefits I experienced from this one practice included improved approachability, increased positivity, empowerment and engagement, decreased turnover, more efficient systems, proactive versus reactive problem solving, transparent and trusting communication, and improved relationships. And when I documented my rounding so that key findings were communicated to senior leaders, our organization had leadership that was more closely connected to day-to-day operations, which benefited decision-making at all levels.

Your employees want a relationship with you that is professional and personal. Rounding with your employees regularly will increase your approachability. The greatest compliment I have ever received as a leader was when an employee would say, "You are so approachable. I can talk to you about anything." I really worked hard at that throughout my leadership career. I wanted to be seen as a leader that my employees could come to and I would problem solve with them, not do something for them or to them. Rounding really was the tool I used to create that approachability. It is the epitome of an "open-door" policy.

Rounding with purpose is key when you want to make your organization a better place to work. If this is a new practice for you, employees are going to wonder, "What the heck is she doing, hauling us in her office every day?" There may come a time when you need to explain your purpose in rounding.

Telling the why might sound something like this: "I really want to make our department a great place for everyone to work. In order to do that, I want to get everyone's thoughts and input on our work environment."

Explaining your purpose and intent for rounding is impactful the very first time you round with your employees. However, if you never follow up on what you learned, or if you never sit down with them one-on-one to round again, they will think that either you were coerced by a senior leader to round or it was the Kool-Aid flavor of the month. It was just another task to you in a long line of management tasks, and you simply cannot get to it again.

Stop the madness! This is too important. Explain the "why" the first few times you round, and the word will get out. Then, make sure you are very systematic in your purposeful rounding. Make a common time and way of scheduling rounding at times that work for you and your employees.

Ask the same questions with just minor variations. With consistency on your part, your employees will develop an understanding that you will be asking for their positives each and every time you round. People like dependability in their work life. Let employees see that you are a leader who behaves, performs, and contributes. Systematic and purposeful is the absolute key. Rounding with forty to fifty of your employees in one week to get rounding off your to-do list is not it.

Leaders can promote positivity through rounding by teaching their team how to shift the challenges they experience into positive outcomes. You will read in our Solution for Recognition, Celebration, and Appreciation that positivity is not an automatic go-to emotion in most people. Positivity is something that has to be practiced.

The technique of rounding really does promote positivity in your work environment, one conversation at a time. It turns around that phenomenon that leaders experience with employees who want to dump all of their misery at your feet every day. When you round with intent and purpose to build relationships, you will automatically promote positivity. The very first question you ask your employee during rounding will turn their brain to positive thoughts, as opposed to, "My job is horrible, and we are too busy!"

Leaders may have an expectation that employees will do what the leader would do in any given situation. Not likely! Empowerment in the workplace is not something that just happens (unless you have a "proceed until apprehended" personality style like some of us). Empowerment is a gift that is given. Let your employees know that they have the power to change things in their work environment. Use rounding as a way to coach them through whatever difficult situation may be challenging them.

Promoting engagement and empowerment through rounding may be as simple as teaching employees how to address equipment needs, how to initiate a work order when something is broken, or how to resolve a conflict with a peer. All of these empowerment tools you place in an employee's toolbox will lessen your leadership workload and also engage the employee to forge ahead in the workplace.

Rounding is also a continual method to assess employee engagement. You don't have to wait for the annual survey to measure this for you; you can assess it daily. Take the pulse of your employee relationships, satisfaction, and engagement.

Through rounding you can lessen the likelihood that you will be surprised and saddened by the resignation of a great employee. I cannot tell you how many times I was blindsided by an employee resignation before I began incorporating rounding into each day.

There is a key difference in the paradigms of leaders versus employees. This perception is unspoken, unless you round daily on your employees. Here is a description of how your employees may *right now* perceive you and your leadership actions: "He is the leader. He knows all and sees all. Surely he must know what I am thinking and feeling and what is going on with me. Can't he see that I am frustrated almost daily by what is going on around here? Doesn't he care? Doesn't he know that I have a lot of job opportunities and that I could leave here anytime?"

Your highest-performing employees do not threaten you with leaving — they often just do it.

Employees want efficient systems. They do not want to redo their work or face barriers that impede their efficiency. Quite simply, if you don't know about it, you cannot fix it. Rounding gets you in the know. Rounding assists in finding creative solutions to breaking down barriers and roadblocks.

Rounding provides leaders with an opportunity to be a transparent and open communicator. Transparency reduces stress and negativity in your employees, no matter the message. Even on those days that you have to deliver bad news to a group of people or an individual that you *have developed a relationship with*, you will gain their respect for the transparent method of communicating that message. Again, a reduction of stress happens because their work life is *known* to them.

Relaying the key findings from your rounding activities up the chain of command to the organization's CEO allows for the senior leaders to be more knowledgeable and in touch with the front lines of day-to-day operations. This provides a significant boon to decision-making and resource allocation, which we will address later.

Rounding is the single most effective tool leaders have to make employees feel appreciated and heard.

Do not be a statistic. Do not be the leader who loses employees because you were clueless about how to create a great employee experience. People often leave their leader, but they also leave their work environments with feelings of being unappreciated and unheard. Stop the cycle. Even if you have low turnover, round to continually make the work environment the best it can possibly be. Make employees proud to be on the team. Stop your personal whirlwind by engaging and empowering your employees through rounding.

Mastering the Skill of Purposeful Employee Rounding

To help aid in your first steps toward making rounding a staple in your work procedure, the initial focus will be on the key questions that are going to get you the biggest bang for your buck. You know your operations, industry, and work environment. Tailor your rounding questions with these things in mind. Also, make sure you phrase or say them in your own fashion. How I ask a question may not be how you would ask a question. It's important that you are comfortable with this tool. I got to the point in my daily rounding practice that I rarely ever had to look at the list of questions or take notes.

Many leaders will say, "You believe that leaders should round daily. How much time should I schedule for this?" I recommend that you schedule an hour every day for rounding. It should not take this long. Your documentation should never take more than five to ten minutes (more on this later), and you will likely get your rounding completed in twenty minutes or so. Getting the feel for the right amount of questions to ask comes with experience. That being said, you really do not want to shove your employees out of your office simply because their "time is up!" Some rounding sessions just simply take longer. And any time you spend engaging in relationship building is a great investment.

A great tip to set yourself up to be successful in rounding with your employees and peers is to tell all new employees about rounding at any new hire orientation or welcome meeting. If you are a senior leader, this sets the expectation that leaders will be rounding with the new employees. As a frontline leader, it is another way to communicate to a new employee (or any employee): "I value you and your role in the department. I want to make this a great work environment and to make you feel appreciated for the work that you do."

Sue and I have been asked many times by leaders at our public training Summits if it is okay to send out rounding questions prior to rounding meetings with employees. Absolutely!

When you first begin the practice of rounding with your employees, there may be some trepidation at being the first few employees to be invited for a "chat." Providing your employees the questions in advance can lessen any fears. Anyone can tell that rounding is a very positive experience just by reading the questions. It will also save time during the rounding as they can prepare their thoughts in advance.

Our recommended key categories of rounding questions can be used in any business, profession, or workplace. Sue and I have even met forest firefighters who round daily with their employees and peers. Tailor it to your profession. Remember that the primary goal is building relationships.

Key Categories of Employee Rounding Questions

- Relationship building

- Expression of gratitude and thankfulness

- Safety in the work environment

- Equipment, supplies, and training/education/certification needs

- Customized questions regarding improvement priorities or goals

- Your leadership: "How am I doing?"

- Gather recognition opportunities

The order in which you ask the questions is vital. You want to sandwich the "meat" of the rounding between two opportunities for employees to express positivity. You will find in the Celebration, Recognition, and Appreciation Solution that positivity in the workplace is something that takes a fair amount of work. Our brains are simply not trained to go to positivity first, and certainly not regularly.

Just like your employees do not act in an empowered way automatically, they do not always experience things with a positive viewpoint. You need to lead them there, and when you round you can set them up for a very positive day simply by starting and ending your rounding with questions that prompt positive responses.

Relationship-Building Question

Relationships are essential to building employee engagement. Rounding is all about strengthening relationships with your employees. You need to show them that you care about them as people.

You may know your employees extremely well. Maybe you think you know everything about them. Yet your relationships with them need to grow and be nurtured. If you know them very well, a great icebreaker or relationship-building question is: "Tell me something about you that I don't already know." Ask them about their children or grandchildren, their day-off activities, or how they are handling a certain situation you may know of.

This is the point in rounding where you will want to interject follow-up from the last time you rounded with them (i.e., "Last time we met, you mentioned…"). Review your past rounding notes in preparation. This really cements you as a caring, communicative, systematic, and purposeful leader who follows through.

Begin Rounding on a Positive Note

My experience in healthcare led me to understand that health-care employees are trained to focus on what is wrong. We look for what's wrong with the patient all the time. In a radiology department, they aren't taking pictures of the patient's normal body parts. An emergency room nurse sitting in the triage chair has three minutes to figure out what is *wrong* with the patient so she can send the patient to the right place. Soon, our whole out-look at work and at home can begin to start with, "What's wrong with this person or situation?"

We need to be intentional about bringing out the posi-tives. The Recognition, Celebration, and Appreciation Solution will overview for you how our minds work and why intentional positivity is a practice that every leader and employee (and all of mankind!) needs to incorporate into their day. When you ask your employees often during rounding what is *right* with their day, your department, or their shift, positive things start to happen.

Choose your way to ask a question that elicits a focus on positivity: "What's good about today? What is working well in our department today? Describe a positive about work today."

Incorporate Leadership Safety Rounds

This is such a proactive leadership tactic. If you always wait for an occurrence, incident, or near-miss report to cross your desk, what have you done? You have allowed bad things to either happen or potentially happen. Your employees are your eyes and ears, and they know what is going on in your department every day.

I admit from personal nursing experience that I did not always take the time to fill out an occurrence report with safety concerns until they were *big* issues. I rarely took the time to report a near miss. But, if a leader asked me what my safety concerns were, I felt relief at being able to express them. Don't just rely on documented safety reports. By the time you get them, you may have a problem that may take weeks or months to resolve. Take care of the safety concerns and issues in your department more concurrently or proactively by rounding.

Again, ask the question in your own way: "Are there any safety issues I need to address? Do you see unsafe work practices happening anywhere? Is there anything keeping you awake at night regarding safety?"

Equipment and Supplies

I don't know about you, but I hated equipment issues as a frontline leader, primarily because it seemed as if a vital piece of needed equipment was either missing, broken, or needed to be replaced *all the time*. This is one of those situations when your employees feel as though you definitely have eyes in the back of your head and you know *exactly* what is going on in your department 24/7. When my emergency room nurses would tell me that an inebriated patient pulled equipment off the wall and broke it *two weeks ago*, I would respond, "People, is my office in Trauma Room 5? Do I work there? I do not. You work there, so please tell me when something is missing or broken in your work space!"

Asking your employees if there are any equipment or supply issues that need to be addressed is essential to your success as a positive, proactive leader for many reasons — the first being that you will learn of equipment issues earlier by asking this question.

A second reason is because you are continuously preparing for your next budget. There will be items that your employees will ask for in rounding that you cannot purchase immediately. But if they are a great idea (even better if they are a revenue generator), let your employee know you need to wait for a new budget cycle to propose to purchase it in the new year. Asking your employees will make sure that great ideas for purchasing new equipment, or updating aging equipment, do not fall through the cracks.

A third, and ever so important, reason is that this is an opportunity to coach on empowerment while you are rounding. Let me explain. If an employee tells you that there is a light bulb at the end of the hall that is continually blinking and he or she is very concerned that someone will have a seizure from looking at it all shift, simply state the following: "Oh my, I do not want that to happen! Have you learned how to submit a work order? Anytime, and I mean *anytime*, anything is broken, I am giving you free rein to call maintenance or file the work order so that they can come and fix it. You do not have to wait for me."

Something else I did for years was to give up sweating the minor equipment and supply details. I had willing employees who were more than happy to make sure we had the right equipment and supplies, in the right place, at the right time. I adored these employees; they made my life and the lives of their peers so much easier. I simply asked the materials management leader if I could assign purchasing authority to these designated employees, and it was so.

As with all rounding questions, phrase the question in your own way: "Do you have the equipment and supplies you need to do your job? Is there a supply we are continuously running out of? Is there a supply we don't have that you wish we did? Is there anything missing or broken that you need in order to do your job today?"

Training, Education, and Certification

Something that Sue and I have noticed as we travel around the country and speak to leaders from hospitals and healthcare organizations of all sizes is that, for whatever reason, the travel and education budget is cut first when budgetary constraints happen. We believe this is the very *last* thing that should be cut. Developing leaders and valuable employees is central to a great organization; however, I am saving this soapbox for another chapter. What I will say now is that when your employees hear that training and education has been frozen once, they may never speak of their hopes and desires for enrichment and growth in their professional lives again. They become apathetic (i.e. "My organization does not invest in me.").

Asking your employees about their training, education, or certification needs allows you to assist employees in developing a career path. This conversation shows that you are supportive of their growth and development. Creating a defined career path is a key driver to employee engagement.

Employees of all generations want to know where they are going and what their role is in the organization. The millennials (the youngest generation which is poised to take the place of the baby boomers in our organizations) see a career path as an extremely important part of their employment.

These rounding questions might be something along the lines of the following: "What training and education do you feel you need? Do you feel as though you received enough education and training on (name the initiative)? Where do you see yourself in five years? Have you ever thought of becoming certified or obtaining an advanced degree?"

The rounding question, "Have you ever thought of becoming certified?" led to quite a discovery with one of my employees. I asked that question one day to a nurse named Pam. Pam was an amazing emergency room nurse. She had ice in her veins during a trauma, and I never stopped admiring her composure. She would take an anesthesiologist by the tie and say, "You, intubate." She would grab a trauma surgeon by her coat, saying, "You, chest tube." And they always did it. Quickly.

Knowing that Pam had already accumulated a laundry list of certifications, I still asked her the rounding question regarding further certifications. Her reply was, "Actually, yes, I am going to be certified. I have signed up for a class to become a real estate agent."

What? I was floored. Pam was my rock star. She was my go-to. I never once imagined she would think of another career as viable. I had always envisioned she would be mentoring a far younger generation of nurses until very late in her life.

She said, "You know, no one is sick enough for me anymore."

Then it hit me. I had been noticing a change in Pam's attitude toward some of the emergency room patients. She wanted the crisis, yet in emergency room nursing, the greater majority of the time you are not dealing with a crisis. And if there is a crisis, it may not always be in your room.

So, we chatted, and I re-recruited her to a hospital that loved her. She became a night shift supervisor, and other leaders could sleep at night knowing Pam was on the job. She needed a new role, and I would not have been able to assist her without rounding and asking the question. She could have sold a big house on the water in beautiful Northern Michigan and been gone! Sue and I call these conversations "pulling someone off the ledge." My point is, you have to round to ask great questions to truly know when you may have an employee on the ledge.

Customized Question(s) Regarding Improvement Priorities or Goals

The need for this question in your rounding may seem obvious. If you work in an environment that is not culturally advanced in problem solving, you may make many decisions on your own as a leader. I do not mean that to be derogatory. If left alone to put a new process or project in place, a leader may not always think of all the angles.

I worked for a long time in a top-down leadership culture and made all decisions about purchasing equipment and writing policies on my own. It was when I discovered a shared governance approach, by working with multidisciplinary teams on projects, that I discovered that all bases were covered when the project or process was rolled out. Your work culture or leadership style simply may not be there yet.

When there is a need to change the work of your employees, it is the best practice to have the people whose work is affected be involved in the decisions. In organizations that are 24/7, involvement of representatives from the "off shifts" should not be passed by as the work flow may be much different on each shift or on certain days like holidays or weekends. These differences should be taken into consideration when designing a great new process.

Early in my leadership, I did not do a great job including the frontline nurses when I was putting a new piece of equipment or work-flow change in place. As I learned, this can be catastrophic!

And even when there is a collaborative process with engaged employees participating, asking rounding questions about current initiatives is highly recommended. In the planning phases of a change, you can ask rounding questions targeted on the new process and how employees feel it will affect their work. After a change has been initiated, ask questions about how the change is going and if there is anything that isn't working as anticipated. Employees may recognize what needs to be done to tweak the process so it works better than originally planned.

The story below describes the importance of asking rounding questions about new initiatives:

Anne-Marie is a legacy nurse, meaning she has been a nurse for a long time. And she has a very direct communication style. She wants deeply to take great care of patients, and it doesn't matter what is placed in front of her, she is going to find a way to make great patient care happen.

One night shift, when I was a fairly new vice president, I was rounding with employees on a large medical-surgical unit. We had just put a high-tech automated pharmacy dispensing system in place, and I wanted to make sure all was well. When I walked into the medication room in this particular nursing unit, I noticed that Anne-Marie was getting medications out of this new pharmacy dispensing system.

"Hi, Anne-Marie. How are things? I am rounding tonight to make sure that the new way of dispensing medication at night is going well for all of you," I said.

Anne-Marie turned to me and said, "You! Was this idiotic machine your idea?"

Uh-oh.

She continued on to say, "I had a patient tonight who was seizing. Do you realize that some idiot has created seventeen steps to get IV Ativan out of this machine? Do you realize that no matter how quick I get at using this machine to get medications I need for my patients, seventeen steps will never be quick enough for a seizing patient?"

Perfect. So glad I showed up in the middle of the night for this conversation. I expected to be lauded as a hero for approving the funds and providing input into the magical machine that was going to make their work lives so much more efficient.

It gets better.

Anne-Marie was showing me how she had fixed the problem that a project team of employees and leaders had "so obviously missed."

"I figured out how to get Ativan out of the machine a lot quicker. And I showed everyone who is working tonight how to do it, too," she told me.

She moved to the back of the machine and flipped a switch, opening every single drawer and refrigerator in the room, thereby negating every medication security, documentation, and charging measure that were important functions of the new system.

Her last words in this conversation: "Please fix this. Tonight!"

With the help of an on-call pharmacist, we did fix it that night. Yet my sense was that if I had not rounded with Anne-Marie that very night, I may not have learned in a timely fashion about that key mistake we had made as the project team that had planned for the use of this new technology.

Feedback on Your Leadership

During rounding, ask your employees about your leadership. Some of you may be thinking, "Are you kidding me? I do not want to hear what employees have to say about my leadership!" Yes, you do! As leaders, we get so little feedback on how we are really, truly doing our job. Who best to know how you are doing as a leader than the employees that you lead?

You may have to build up to this question. For instance, I used to say to my employees, "You are so lucky because we survey our patients, and they tell you how you are doing. I also need someone to give me feedback on how I can improve in my role. I really do value your opinion and want to be a better leader for you."

You might want to be specific in asking about things you've done recently as the leader. You could ask, "How did I do with (insert your action here—e.g., the Christmas schedule, a new piece of equipment, a new policy)? Did I communicate this effectively?"

What your employees will say at first when you start rounding with them and ask a question such as "How am I doing as your leader?" is that you are "fine." Fine? FINE? Seriously? You are a visionary leader. You have strategy burning in your soul. You love your job. Fine? At my house, *fine* is a four-letter word. Fine means, "Go change that dress because your butt looks HUGE in it." Anyone who thinks my cooking is fine doesn't eat for a week. I despise "fine." Don't settle for fine in your leadership. Dig a bit deeper. Tell your employees that you really, truly want to be a great leader. What do they think you need to do to get there?

Gather Recognition Opportunities

Gathering recognition opportunities is the positive note with which you will end the rounding. You are going to stroke the positive chord again in your employees by asking them if there is anyone they work with who should be recognized. Again, your employees will at first be very confused about how to reach for positivity. It takes a few sessions of rounding before they really dig deep for answers to this.

At first, they may say, "Oh, I don't know. Everybody does a great job here." Or, "Well, I knew you were going to ask me this, but I can never think of someone to thank when you ask me." Let them think about it and email you back, but put a tickler somewhere. Do not let them get away without recognizing a fellow coworker.

Your employees may also want to thank the same people over and over. When I was rounding with my intensive care unit employees, we had just started working with a critical care specialist for the first time. The nurses loved working with him and all wanted me to send him a thank-you note each week. Finally, I had to say, "The doctor's wife is going to key my car. Who else can we thank?" Encourage your employees to thank someone outside of their own department. The brain functions better when thinking or stating positivity. You want your employees to leave the rounding with their brains all lit up from positivity!

"Burning Questions" for Senior Leadership

While asking employees if they have any questions that can be answered by senior leadership isn't always adopted as part of a leader's rounding, we mention it here for organizations that may want to consider this tactic. Asking this question has a purpose that is key to organizational-wide transparency and engagement.

It is a great question to add to rounding if your organization can develop a process for the employees' burning questions to be posed to senior leadership, and then have the questions and answers communicated throughout the entire organization. It makes sense that if one employee has a question for senior leadership to answer, many more likely do too. Encourage them to know they can ask you anything about their place of employment, and you will get those answers.

Follow-Up and Follow-Through from Rounding Builds Trust

When you round with employees, there are so many positive effects. When you document and communicate the key findings from rounding, you gain additional benefits.

Your documentation serves many people, starting with employees. You document your rounding so that the next time you are rounding with an employee, you can close the loop on the previous conversation. You can make statements like, "The last time we talked, you were concerned about the safety of the new patient lifts, and I called the equipment representative. Did the training he provided make you feel better about using this equipment?"

It may be three months since your last rounding with this employee, but they will be so very impressed that you remembered their concern. Remember, rounding is a tool for you to make your employees feel appreciated and heard. This increases their engagement and decreases your turnover.

Others that benefit from the documentation of rounding are the organization's CEO and senior leaders. Having served as a senior leader, I was more effective and proactive (as was the CEO) when leaders rounded and documented their rounding in a format the CEO and I could see in a timely fashion.

The CEO position is a difficult one. There are so many people vying for the CEO's time and attention. When leaders round and document their rounding, it keeps the senior leaders connected to the operations of their organization. Operations is the pulse. Systematic and purposeful rounding is a frequent checking of the pulse. The senior leaders will know what is going on in various departments, what the equipment needs are, who the ROCKSTAR high performers are, and what burning questions employees have for the senior leadership team.

I know for certain that I was a much better vice president because my frontline leaders rounded. I also know that the CEO was a much better CEO and felt better about his role and connectedness to his hospital as a result of rounding and the timely documentation he received.

Freshly armed with the knowledge of operations, this CEO walked the hallways of the hospital engaging others in more meaningful ways. He would greet employees with, "Tough night last night in intensive care? Sounds like you guys did a great job getting that patient airlifted quickly." As he was in line getting his breakfast in the cafeteria, he would say, "Thanks so much for providing a courtesy food and beverage cart for the family members who had to stay here all weekend with their sick child. I know they really appreciated it." Employees would be staring at him when he left their area saying, "How does he know all that?"

While rounding documentation is beneficial and serves many people, leaders all over the country tell Sue and me that the documentation piece is where they struggle. This documentation struggle may be what prevents them from even adopting the practice of rounding.

Keep Rounding Documentation Simple

- Keep the focus of documentation on key findings that are important for future reference and for senior leaders to be aware of.

- Documentation should not take you more than five or ten minutes to complete.

- Make sure that this process allows you to retrieve past rounding documentation easily in the future.

- The process should ensure that the documentation will reach senior leaders in a timely fashion.

Find the easiest way to document for you. Some organizations will have a computerized or other method already in place. Provide input into making sure it works for you. This is very important to your success.

If there is not a system in place, you may simply develop a Word document as a template of your rounding questions. Just type your key findings into the template, attach it in an email to senior leaders, and make sure you save it in a folder labeled with the employee's name. Handwritten rounding logs are okay if your writing is legible. Handwritten logs can be copied and delivered, faxed, or scanned and emailed to senior leaders (on the same day!). When I was a hospital leader, our CEO was so committed to his leaders being able to document efficiently, he paid for the medical transcriptionists to transcribe the rounding reports dictated daily by leaders. Again, seek out options to effectively and efficiently document, and do what works for you.

If documentation is taking longer than five to ten minutes, you may want to review the content of your documentation. If it takes a long time for you to document, it takes a long time for your senior leaders to review. Keep the documentation concise and focus on the key findings.

What your senior leaders do not want to see in a rounding documentation:

- That you perceived a meeting you attended as a rounding and documented the rounding like meeting minutes.

- That you wrote down everything that you did for the day so senior leaders would know how busy you are.

- That you only document what you need or the trouble you are having, never the positives from rounding. A leader who worked for me would do that in her rounding documentation. The very thing she had been in my office for on Monday that I had said no to became the focal point of her rounding documentation sent to the CEO for the rest of the week. Your senior leader and CEO need positives, too. Trust me, their days are filled with very little positive too much of the time.

Just as you make employee rounding a habit in your day, you need to make the documentation a habit, too. If the documentation is an afterthought or something you try to squeeze in, it likely isn't going to happen. Plan for it. Schedule it. Make it part of your daily routine.

Beyond the documentation is the follow-up to what you learned from rounding. The very best piece of advice I received regarding follow-up is to do the good stuff first. It's kind of like eating your dessert first at dinnertime. You deserve a little positivity in your life as well, so whatever recognition and appreciation your employees asked you to provide, get it done first. Write a thank-you note, send an email, make a phone call, go out and provide public recognition. Whatever it is you feel is best to demonstrate appreciation, do it. It makes the rest of your follow-up so much better!

Acquire suggested supplies and equipment or put them on your budget-planning list. Communicate any purchases to your employees. Publicly thank the employee who gave you the suggestion during rounding. Likewise, coordinate suggested training or education. Communicate to employees that the training is in follow-up to a suggestion received through rounding.

In follow-up to rounding, you may need to implement action steps to repair a major system issue. This may not be within your scope or authority to make happen overnight. It may take the efforts of many people and departments. My Anne-Marie story took an entire group of leaders and employees sitting down and looking at what other roadblocks and barriers we had put in the way of effective patient care with our project. It is important to communicate to all of your employees the steps that have been taken in follow-up, even if they are not done by you or take a longer period of time to complete.

You need to find a way to report back to your department what things are being improved upon based on employee input received during rounding (see Stoplight Report Example in Appendix 3). The Stoplight Report is an easy-to-read report that provides an effective way to communicate with employees. It summarizes the status of issues identified by employees and communicated during rounding. Make sure you update the Stoplight Report as the status of issues change, or at least once a month. Have the report saved on your computer so you can easily update it consistently and then post the updated version monthly. Post it everywhere—your employee bulletin board, near the time clock, the bathroom door—everywhere!

How you document and follow through is central to effective, purposeful, and systematic rounding that leads to amazing benefits. It is so important to close the loop on this valuable time you have spent with your employees.

If you view rounding as another task that has been put upon you, your employees will feel that. Even if you may not have been your most approachable, charismatic self during the actual rounding process, your follow-through and follow-up will still convey the importance of engaging employees. We have so few opportunities in leadership to give careful consideration to trust building when we are making decisions on the fly all day. Make sure you build this trust by following up and following through on your rounding.

Senior Leader Rounding

Senior leaders impart a vision for where the organization is going. They infuse pride in what the organization is achieving. When your employees are asked where they work, they likely do not state their department; they state their organization. The pride that they carry when saying this is so important to turning each employee into a "Chief Marketing Officer" in your community.

Employees want to know that their senior leaders are there for them. While frontline employees and senior leaders may not develop a relationship close enough to know what motivates both parties, they want a relationship based on respect and approachability.

Many senior leaders have created time in their schedules for "management by wandering around." This is not purposeful rounding. Senior leaders have the responsibility to communicate the mission and vision of the organization and connect how current events are in alignment with the strategy of the organization. The interactions of the CEO and other senior leaders with employees are very important. Senior leadership should be prepared for their time rounding with employees and should avoid the urge to act as a hero to solve problems for employees and frontline leaders. Senior leader rounding is not a rescue mission.

The frequency of senior leader rounding is often less than that of frontline leaders. Even though senior leaders may have many direct reports, their meeting schedule and commitments often limit their availability to create daily time for rounding. Senior leaders rounding once a week, coupled with staying connected to the day-to-day operations by reading rounding documentation of frontline leaders, is often sufficient.

If your organization has a standard rounding time established, this is a great time for senior leaders to be in departments rounding and validating that rounding is happening. I had lunch at a conference once with a vice president who worked in a hospital system in Texas with twenty thousand employees. Their organization established weekly "sacred time" that was blocked time in which all leaders engaged in rounding. There were no meetings held throughout the entire organization ever during sacred time. The senior leadership team focused on being out of their offices and being visible in various departments as they conducted rounding. And, if a leader sent an email un-related to rounding during this time, it was duly noted (not in a good way!) that this leader was not spending his or her time rounding with employees as he or she should have been. The designated sacred time created an accountability system and was a testament to the organization's commitment to building relationships with employees.

When Sue became the chief nursing officer for the second time in the same hospital, she wanted to get to know the nursing employees again. She would dedicate sacred time in the nursing departments to do this. As frontline leaders, we would assist by scheduling employees that were working that day to round with her, each for just fifteen minutes or so. During this time, she was really checking the pulse of the overall nursing services, and making sure employees knew her and knew that she cared about their work environment. She would ask questions about equip-ment and supplies, their understanding of a capital project, and whether or not my leadership was well received and effective. And, of course, she gathered positive stories so she could extend appreciation and write thank-you notes.

Senior leaders can accomplish what Sue did by round-ing in a different department weekly. The senior leader should schedule this time with the leader of that department so prepa-ration can take place (e.g., the CEO may round with an employ-ee who has just been disciplined...the CEO should know about this in advance). A brief standardized report format may help prepare the senior leader for rounding. This brief report or con-versation could include these highlights about the department:

- Recent accomplishments

- New equipment

- Employees to recognize

- Employees to coach/mentor

- Tough questions/issues

- Other goal results (employee satisfaction, quality/ safety, growth, finance, etc.)

- Other "heads-up" issues

Sue and I also recommend that frontline leaders "invite" the CEO into their departments to round with employees with a very specific purpose in mind (e.g., recognition regarding a specific goal accomplishment, to learn about an improved process, to focus on a key safety initiative, etc.). And, if you are having a celebration in your department, invite the CEO to stop in. Allow the CEO the opportunity to experience positivity in his or her day as well.

Interdepartmental Leader Rounding

Frontline leaders have a unique ability to break down silos in an organization by rounding with the employees who work in other departments. It is great to ask: "How can our department help you to serve our customers better?" Almost every time that

Sue and I enter a new partner hospital for the first time to do an assessment of their patient and employee experience, as well as their culture, we hear employees say, "We have silos here."

It has gotten to the point that we have developed a training session titled, "SILO is a Four-Letter Word!" A healthy culture is a positive and blameless culture. Breakdown happens between departments when there are misperceptions or misunderstandings that lead to blame. There simply cannot be blame in a healthy culture.

When misperceptions or miscommunications happen, causing tension between departments, the employees involved often do not take the time to work out their differences. They just pass the blame on to the next person. Pretty soon it is an "always" or "never" blame (e.g., "Radiology *never* tells us when they put a patient back in his or her room. We *always* have to wait for our labs longer than we should.").

Leaders have the ability, through purposeful interdepartmental rounding, to break down those imaginary blaming walls between departments by actively listening without getting defensive and taking action based on the other department's needs. Effective leader rounding in departments other than those you manage can really make a difference in letting others see that your department really does want to create effective work systems. Through rounding, we can build collaboration, not silos.

A frontline leader who garners opportunities for interdepartmental recognition can create a bond between employees in other departments. For example, if a registered nurse asks you to thank one of the support department employees for a job well done, you now have an opportunity through recognition to create positive feelings between the registered nurse and this other employee. That is one way in which silos are broken down.

Early in our years of rounding, Sue and I noticed that most interdepartmental rounding was focused on leaders of support departments rounding with the employees in the departments that they support. In recent years, we have encouraged interdepartmental rounding between any and all departments that interact day-to-day to get the job done. The expanded use of interdepartmental rounding makes great sense given the prevalence of silos and work environment issues that cross departmental boundaries.

What Is a Support Leader?

There may be leaders in the organization who manage processes or programs, but not a lot of people. Or, they may oversee the department and group of employees that have their hands on the people who have their hands on the customer. They are the support structure that maintains the behind-the-scenes activities.

They are the wind beneath our wings. Whenever I had the opportunity to speak to a group of new hospital employees, I always told them, "Just as it takes a village to raise a child, it takes a village to run a hospital. A hospital is not made up of just clinicians, as is often thought by those outside the healthcare profession. It is made up of plumbers, floor waxers, accountants, cooks, and pharmacists. We have so many amazing, diverse jobs here, and every single one of you has one thing in common: the patient and serving our community. All of you are important, and not one doctor or nurse could do their job each day without you doing yours well."

Leaders of support departments should round each day, focusing on rounding with their employees and also employees in the departments they support and interact with.

As with employee rounding, Sue and I believe that any leader can adopt the practice of interdepartmental rounding even if the entire organization does not. In organizations that move forward with adopting rounding as a leadership responsibility, there will be quite a few conversations that will go on between the leaders regarding how much rounding is required. The initial focus should be on *all* leaders adopting the systematic practice of purposeful rounding, not necessarily the quantity of rounding by each leader.

Yet, I remember those days of debate about leaders who had to do more. Unfortunately, because we wanted rounding to be "equal" we created more silos between leaders. Rounding is not equal. Leaders who have more employees will likely round more than those leaders with fewer employees. It is a simple math equation. Every leader in the organization needs to work to create a great environment for each and every employee, and leaders differ in the number of employees they lead.

Therefore, Sue and I advocate that even those leaders whose calendars are quite full still need to round in other departments. And here is why. As a leader of a large department with many employees, you still have other areas in the organization that you rely on for their services. Either another department serves your employees and customers or you serve theirs. Give that some thought as you are creating a rounding schedule to keep yourself organized with employee and interdepartmental rounding. You will likely need to prioritize to make this possible.

Start with identifying the two or three key departments that your department interacts with and/or has the biggest opportunities to improve collaboration. Where are the silos? Do not leave those departments off your rounding list. Even if you have created an amazing work environment for your employees to work in every day, you did not create a bubble. Your employees need collaboration with the outside to get things done; make sure they have a barrier-free way to get that assistance.

Below you can see the types of questions that are helpful in interdepartmental rounding. While you wouldn't want to ask all of the questions in the list below in each rounding session, you will want to follow the guidance to start and end the rounding with positivity. Likely, four to five of the rounding questions for each interdepartmental rounding session will be just what is needed to build collaboration.

Sample of Interdepartmental Rounding Questions

- Can you describe a recent situation in which our departments (or members of our departments) worked well together to serve a patient? Or fix a problem? Or improve something?

- Can you describe a recent situation in which our departments didn't work well together?

- What are the top one or two things we do that make it difficult for you to do your job?

- If you were running our department, what would you do differently?

- If we were easier to work with, what would that look like?

- Customized question(s) focused on a current/recent happening (e.g., Since we've changed X, how has this impacted your department? We are working on X change. What input do you have on this?)

- When you need something from our department, can you count on us? Are we there when you need us?

- Is there someone in my department who I can recognize for doing a great job?

- Anything else I should know or any further questions?

As with employee rounding, you will want to document the key findings from your interdepartmental rounding. And, all the previous advice about good follow-up and follow-through applies here, too.

How Often Should I Round?

It's worth repeating that the initial focus should be on *all* leaders in the organization adopting the systematic practice of purposeful rounding, not necessarily the quantity of rounding by each leader. That being said, we are often asked for recommendations regarding how much rounding a leader should do.

Our general recommendation is that you round each day

you work. The reason we advocate for daily rounding is that in order to see effective results, you have to round often and with real purpose. You do not lose weight by watching the foods you put in your mouth *sometimes*, or by starving yourself one week a month. Nor should you round in this way.

Rounding needs to become an easy, natural part of your day that you cannot imagine giving up. Just like exercise. When you start exercising every day, you will feel as though something is missing from the natural rhythm of your day when you skip it. You will feel really bad when you skip it for a week, like something really big is missing from your life. That is how important purposeful rounding is to your leadership.

One way to aid in your efforts to make it a daily habit is to keep track. Keeping track is good for accountability, but it also helps you to reflect on which of your employees and which departments you are rounding with — or not rounding with. It may be tempting to always round with those "rock star" employees. You know, those employees who always make you feel good with every interaction you have? You will tend to gravitate toward them if you do not keep track of your employees that you have rounded with and those you have missed. The same can be true when we avoid interdepartmental rounding with departments that are the most problematic. Hold yourself accountable to get at the tough stuff.

Do not forget about making time for your employees working the off-shifts and weekends. Maybe you will have to adjust your schedule to meet with them, or they may be willing to come in on their day off to get some one-on-one time with their leader.

When pressed by leaders and organizations to recommend

a number, Sue and I advocate that leaders with a large span of direct control, or twenty-five or more direct reports, round with each of their employees once a quarter. A smaller span of control, or less than twenty-five direct reports, should be rounded with monthly. Those are the numbers that we give to senior leaders when they ask us for a way to validate, by number, the amount of rounding their leaders should be doing.

These guidelines for the quantity of employee rounding are the starting point; most organizations that adopt the practice of rounding extend this practice to interdepartmental employees, senior leaders, key stakeholders (e.g., physicians, community members), and customers.

For instance, we know of hospitals that require their leaders to round with community members asking questions prepared to get community input on key areas of their strategy. In hospitals, leaders also round with patients to validate that great care is happening, and with physicians to build relationships and promote collaboration.

If you are not a healthcare leader, you obviously won't have physicians to round with; yet, likely in your profession you have those key stakeholders that are present in your building or that work with your employees every day. Determine who these key stakeholders are and consider if it would be beneficial to put a form of rounding in place to build relationships with them as well.

If you are a healthcare leader, we've included a supplement at the end of this solution dedicated to the important process of rounding with physicians. It might provide benefit to non-healthcare leaders as they consider rounding with important key stakeholders.

Purposeful rounding, of various types, should be the most

important part of your day. It should not be considered simply a task to check off your to-do list, as extra work, or a meaningless quota to meet. Round often, yet round with purpose and with heart.

When Should I Round?

When to round can vary based on the type of organization or the individual department. When I was a frontline leader, the volume of activity in the department was lower in the morning, so I always rounded as soon as I got to work. This also meant that I could round with employees from the day and night shifts.

When I became the chief nursing officer, I scheduled rounding on my calendar by being mindful of optimal times in the various departments.

Then when I became a frontline leader in a very large department, I needed to get creative about my rounding schedule. There were 120 employees in my department, so I could not round quarterly with every employee while they were at work. Afternoons were the best times for rounding with employees during work. Yet, often I had to contact employees and make appointments with them to come in on their day off, or I appeared (magically) on the night shift.

It's very important that whenever you round, you provide very open, clear, and transparent communication about what you are doing. Asking an employee to join you in your office can be very scary for them and leaves everyone else wondering, "Who is going to the boss's office next?"

You want employees to feel as positive about rounding as you do. You want your employees to see rounding as the way you lead proactively and efficiently. They will want to help you in that, as it benefits them tremendously.

Make sure you remember who you are serving in this process. In order for rounding to be purposeful, you need to do it at a time when employees will not worry about the work they are leaving undone.

Although it is important for you to create a natural rhythm that incorporates rounding, documentation, and follow-up into your daily work, you need to exercise your best judgment about when.

Optimally, rounding should be scheduled whenever you can. When time for rounding is blocked off on your schedule, it needs to be valued as sacred time to you and others. In other words, others need to know they cannot automatically schedule over rounding at the first sign of a scheduling conflict.

A Story about Kathleen

Kathleen was the human resources department leader in our organization at a time when Sue and I were both senior leaders. Kathleen has many, many years of human resource experience all over the globe and in many different agencies. She is *brilliant*. I have learned so much about leadership from her. When you consider how very busy this type of leader is in a rapidly growing organization, you may have thought that Kathleen would not take kindly to an organization-wide commitment to daily rounding. Not so. Kathleen is a "walk the talk" leader. She truly does believe that as leaders we are to set a great example.

Kathleen led a very busy department and seemed to never get to leave her chair to round in other departments of our organization. This did not stop her. She developed the best practice of doing interdepartmental rounding by making it work for her in her own way. When an employee would call her with a request to meet with her, she would say, "Of course, I have time on my calendar this week. Do you mind if I ask you some rounding questions while we have our time together?"

When she did this, the employee came with the knowledge that they were entering into a professional meeting between two colleagues. Yes, the employee's issue that prompted the meeting was discussed and addressed with the added benefit of rounding, which promotes positivity.

Call to Action

I knew long before an employee engagement survey came out that I had higher employee engagement in my department as a result of my purposeful rounding. Rounding had led to a work environment filled with loyal employees that really, genuinely loved their jobs and each other. Employees were coming to me all the time to talk about improvements they felt we had an opportunity to make. Most of the time, they had already taken the first steps in making those improvements; they just wanted to tell me about them! Rounding can make this happen in your work environment, too.

Just start! Do not wait for a senior leadership blessing.

Do not wait for your organization to make purposeful rounding something every leader is required to do. Start applying what you know and figure it out as you go.

Only you can make this difference, and the difference you will make will be huge. You will be the small pebble that causes a ripple effect all over your organization.

One rounding, one employee at a time.

Rounding Success Plan

Evaluate Current State

- Seek out any existing recommendations or requirements for leaders to conduct rounding. Evaluate any applicable documentation processes. If rounding is required by the organization, seek out leaders who are the "internal champions" of rounding and interview them.

- Seek out any education/training programs that are made available to leaders in the organization to learn about rounding.

- Review the most recent employee survey data and comments, looking for specific survey statements that relate to the benefits of rounding (e.g., "I feel listened to."; "My leader is an effective communicator."; "I have the necessary equipment to do my job."; "I feel informed about what is happening in my department or the hospital."; "I feel that my ideas are considered."; "I feel appreciated for the work I do.").

- Reflect on your personal leadership in the past year. Are you a proactive leader striving to engage employees and create an amazing employee experience and peak results? How are your relationships with your employees? How can rounding improve your leadership?

- Review the employee turnover rate. Review exit interviews, if available. Assess for a realistic view of why employees leave.

Plan and Make Improvements— Select and Prioritize Based on Assessment

- Commit (or recommit) to rounding. Or, refresh your rounding with a focus on becoming more systematic and purposeful.

- Expand your rounding habit into new types of rounding (e.g., interdepartmental).

- Develop an improved process for documentation of your rounding, including communication to applicable senior leaders.

- Develop improved processes for consistent follow-up and follow-through. Incorporate a variation of the Stoplight Report.

- Improve your scheduling and tracking system so that you are consistently rounding with all of your employees (not avoiding certain employees, or certain shifts or groups). Emphasize to those who vie for time on your schedule or can change your schedule (e.g., administrative assistants) that rounding is sacred time.

- **Organization Change Agent:** Advocate for an organization-wide rounding plan for leaders. Develop a system of training, support, and accountability for this change.

Evaluate and Adjust

- Assess how you "feel" about your job after a period of rounding consistently for two to three months. Do you feel more purposeful and proactive in your work? Are employees bringing forth solutions and not just concerns and complaints? Does it feel as though the whirlwind visits you only a few times a week instead of a few times an hour? What has happened to the level of positivity in the work environment? Is silo behavior diminishing?

- Evaluate employee survey and exit interview results. Continue to monitor turnover rates. Conduct mini-surveys of your employees (see the Solution on Measuring and Improving the Employee Experience for ideas) at more frequent intervals than the organization-wide employee surveys.

- Change up your rounding questions from time to time based on priority areas that have been identified for improvement.

- Regularly reassess to evaluate if the changes are leading to improvements. Adjust plan and improvement activities as necessary. See Solution Twelve for guidance.

Supplement—Physician Rounding

Physician rounding is a proactive form of leadership. The reasons are many, but here are two.

Leaders ask many things of physicians all day long. We ask them to assist us with our quality and service initiatives. We ask them to document a certain way and shape their workday around the inner workings of our departments. We want them to discharge their patients in a timely fashion. We want them to treat our employees well and to assist us in creating an amazing work environment. Yet, what do we give back to them? Maybe a jar of nuts on Doctor's Day.

The second reason physician rounding is a very proactive form of leadership is the fundamental way busy physicians communicate to others. Physicians will often see things that could be changed in their work environment (e.g., your department) and then communicate it to whomever happens to be within earshot. The perception of physicians is that your employees are running to you with every point they've made.

Meanwhile, your employees have enough of their own priorities and concerns to deal with. Employees often assume that the physician will be coming to you, the leader, directly with their issues. I have no idea why, but the department leader and physician relationship is such a unique one. As leaders, we have the ability to assist greatly in what they need done, yet they never seem to come to us readily with their ideas. Instead, they get frustrated enough to yell at the brand-new nurse at two o'clock in the morning. "I have been telling everyone about this problem, and nobody's doing anything about it!" You can prevent this from happening. Be proactive in your leadership by rounding with physicians.

You have heard of "happy wife, happy life." The same thing applies to physicians. Like your employees, they are human, and humans want to feel appreciated and heard. They do not, however, view themselves as employees, even if employed by your organization.

Physician rounding is very similar to employee rounding. I was so fortunate in my career as a frontline leader to have two specialties in which I worked directly with a close-knit group of physicians. I led an inpatient oncology department and an emergency department. A certain team of physicians were consistently working with my employees. I wanted to be a collaborator with these physicians. I let them know that I viewed them as leaders in our department as well and that they had just as much responsibility as I did in creating an amazing environment for our employees and patients.

When I rounded with them, I let them know of the "big things" going on around the hospital, and I included them on some employee coaching needs when I thought it would prove helpful to patient care. I was very proactive with the physicians. I wanted them to see me as someone they could trust with the efficient management of the department where they worked and where their patients received care.

When I became the chief nursing officer and then the leader of an inpatient unit with every physician on staff present in the many departments I led, it was another story. Then, my physician rounding took a turn. There were lots of them and only one of me.

The first issue in effective physician rounding is time. Often it is difficult to round with physicians without having a scheduled time. This may actually require setting a meeting time with them. And this is likely most convenient for them before the start of their day, during their lunch hour, or after their office hours. If you are going to round with them without a scheduled appointment time, you would definitely want to ask if they have the time.

We suggest that clinical leaders round with one physician per week if possible. If you are a clinical services leader with a physician who actually works right in your department (e.g., radiology or lab), round with your physicians monthly. If you are a surgical services leader, again, make sure the surgeons know you will be rounding with them quarterly if they are a large group.

The senior leadership team may also participate in making sure that every single physician is rounded with. This can be done by asking individual physicians to meet with the entire senior leadership team at once. In this manner, each senior leader would ask about the effectiveness of the processes and care provided in their department.

You do not want to inundate your physicians with leaders clamoring to round with them. Physician rounding needs to be given careful consideration prior to hard and fast rules for leaders being set. It takes some organization, for sure.

My experience with physician rounding was a very positive one. Physicians go to school for a long time. And when they do, they go to school in many, many other hospitals. Those hospitals have many incredible practices that your physicians can bring to you in the form of standing-order sets, work-process improvements, equipment ideas, and more. Capture their ideas through rounding and respond to them.

Sue and I jokingly subscribe to and promote the "C.A.S.E." (Copy and Steal Everything) method. We challenge you to make it yours, and make it better! The premise is that there are brilliant helpful people all around us with amazing ideas on how to make work environments and care better and to get the work done faster. Reinventing the wheel makes for a long and stressful career. Physicians are no exception. They are brilliant people who likely trained and worked in a dozen or so different healthcare environments before they got to yours. C.A.S.E. what they bring to you.

Rounding proved helpful in creating an improved trauma protocol for the emergency room that I led. Our hospital recruited a fabulous new surgeon. Our emergency department treated a lot of trauma annually as northern Michigan is a great playground for outdoor recreation, but with that comes accidents. This particular surgeon was getting more and more frustrated with how trauma was being managed in her new place of work, and she was routinely expressing that to my employees. When I finally rounded with her, she had reached her boiling point. "We do a poor job of managing trauma. It is not at all how I was trained, and I hate being called in to this chaos."

I said, "You have special training in trauma? Do tell." She proceeded to pull out a trauma protocol she had been carrying around in her briefcase since her arrival. She was simply waiting for someone to ask her or an opportunity to speak with the right person about it.

When our team worked with her to create a new trauma response protocol, and then she led drills on how it would work, her vision unfolded in front of us. In the end, instead of a physician angered all the time by her surroundings, she became a leader, a collaborator, and a partner in efficient, great care. It all started with one rounding session and the question, "Do you have the tools and equipment you need to do your job?"

Suggested Physician Rounding Questions:

- First, thank them for the work that they do to care for patients.

- What is working well?

- Any safety issues/concerns? Do physicians feel safe knowing patients are in the care of employees when they leave at night?

- What two or three things can we do to improve the quality of care to your patients?

- Does the admission (referral, scheduling, etc.) process go well?

- Any supplies, equipment, space, and/or training needs?

- Any burning questions for senior leadership? Anything that leadership can do to improve communication to physicians?

- Are you satisfied with the responsiveness of leaders when you have an issue, concern, or suggestion?

- Is there an employee and/or physician you would like to recognize and why?

- Anything else I should know or any further questions?

Direct Dialogue: Performance Feedback Conversations

You don't have to be a leader for very long to notice that there is variation in how your employees behave, perform, and contribute. Providing feedback, positive or constructive, is a key skill to master when you are leading a team to achieving great results. It is about not just mastering the skill, *but mustering the will* when it comes to providing performance feedback. Could you imagine the coach of a championship team avoiding providing feedback to his or her players?

Some performance feedback will be more formal, such as annual performance evaluations. Additional performance feedback comes in the form of day-to-day conversations. This solution will explore what we term "Direct Dialogue." These are those day-to-day conversations that leaders must have to provide positive, coaching, or constructive feedback. Frequent high-quality feedback is required for individuals and teams to reach peak performance.

A couple of years ago, Jane and I traveled from our homes in the Midwest to Los Angeles to attend public speaking training. We spent two days engrossed in gaining deeper understanding, as well as being intensely critiqued. What we didn't expect when venturing into this training was how much of our time would be spent learning about human interaction.

Ingrained in us while attempting to perfect our public speaking skills was a deeper understanding of several important elements common in human interaction:

1. The most powerful conversations take place one-on-one, face-to-face.

2. A conversation (and, over time, a series of conversations) forms the relationship. One conversation at a time you are maintaining, building, diminishing, or maybe even destroying a relationship.

3. You must consider the effect or reaction you desire from each conversation.

4. The conversation isn't only about the words but the silence and the gestures.

Performance feedback from a leader is truly just a conversation, or series of conversations. Even though leaders have a lifetime of experience in conversing, it is with regular frequency that leaders reach out to us for advice on what to say to their employees.

You can probably guess that those "tough" conversations are the ones in which leaders seek out our assistance. Even the most experienced leaders can struggle with conversations that need to happen when an employee is not behaving, performing, or contributing at the level required.

Sometimes the assistance that a leader needs with a tough conversation is related to knowing the words to say. We will touch on this later in the solution. Let's start with the most common reason that leaders seek out help for tough conversations: building the courage to have them. Leaders may know what to say and may know that it needs to be said, but mustering the will to have the conversation is a different matter entirely.

Mustering the Will

Bearing in mind that a face-to-face conversation is powerful and can impact a relationship, leaders can often struggle with initiating this type of conversation. We often have these thoughts running around in our heads regarding the potentially horrible outcome or reaction that may follow. Our thoughts may trick us into avoiding or minimizing the need to have a difficult conversation. Most commonly, we want to escape an uncomfortable situation. Yes, some performance feedback conversations are uncomfortable for both parties.

Maybe you will recognize some of these thoughts from a time when you were faced with an employee performance or behavior issue:

- I think I'll just be patient and see if the employee will figure this out on his or her own. He or she must know that this is an issue, right?

- What if the employee quits? We are already short-staffed.

- Maybe if I am subtle and hint about this issue, he or she will catch on.

- Maybe it isn't that bad.

- What if I'm wrong about the issue?

- What if he or she gets defensive? Or retaliates?

- It's really not going to make a difference. He or she is not going to change no matter what I say.

- I'll deal with it if it happens again.

- Why bother? Human Resources won't support me anyway.

- The employee is technically competent, so why should I get so concerned about his or her behavior?

- Last time I did this, it didn't go so well. I'm not sure I want to go there again.

- What if he or she perceives me as unfair or mean?

- What if he or she creates a stir afterward?

- Do I really want to open this can of worms?

- If I ignore it, maybe the problem will go away.

- I don't get paid enough to do this.

- The thought of having this conversation makes me sick.

As the above thoughts point to, we often don't want to risk looking bad, making things worse, or doing damage to ourselves or our relationships. Although there are no guarantees, and it does take courage, each of us knows deep within us that we'll be fine. Upon deeper reflection we realize that avoiding important conversations rather than having them is often way more damaging to us, our relationships, and everyone around us. Like public speaking, the fear may be real but the threat often is not.

So, how do we overcome fear of delivering important feedback? We can apply similar advice that we learned from public speaking training:

1. Do it more; and

2. Be prepared.

To overcome your fear, take every opportunity you get, and always be prepared.

Avoiding difficult conversations will never lead you to mastering this skill. Skimping on preparation for these conversations will not set you up for success. So, the tactic we recommend for leaders to gain the courage to have these conversations is to commit to having them and commit to being prepared for them.

In your efforts you may want to engage an accountability buddy. This would be someone with whom you are comfortable admitting your fear of these conversations. This person would be someone you trust to help you prepare for these conversations. This person should be someone who will encourage you to have these conversations even when you are trying to talk yourself out of it and with whom you can debrief after the conversations.

58

After each conversation, you will gain confidence and courage to enter future conversations that may be uncomfortable. Though you may never feel totally comfortable or excited, with practice you will become more successful at achieving desired outcomes with these conversations.

Master the Skill

Providing performance feedback in a formal or informal way is a skill to master. The best coaches don't just know the game, they know their people, and they know how to provide them feedback. When it comes to creating relationships that flourish, the research on the three-to-one positivity ratio guides us as leaders to focus three times more on positive feedback as we do constructive, or negative, feedback.

In this solution, we will overview three types of performance feedback conversations: Complimenting, Coaching, and Correcting.

Direct Dialogue: Complimenting

With this ratio in mind, let's get on to mastering the skill of conversations starting with praise and recognition. These below tactics may be best summarized as "common sense, yet not commonly practiced," which is why leaders often fall short on the three-to-one positivity ratio.

I have worked with leaders who struggled with providing positive feedback as much as they did having those difficult constructive conversations. They admitted to feeling tongue-tied when initiating positive feedback, or, they straight-out admitted to not noticing opportunities to provide positive feedback.

So, before you just breeze over this next section, stop for a moment and reflect on the amount of positive feedback that you provide in a given day, and likely you will find a need to read, and reread, this next section.

Learn to notice what is going right.

Our brains are trained to look for negativity. We spend too much time ruminating over negative events. Our brains do not first reach for positivity in most situations. This is something you can train your brain to do. We'll dive into this more in Solution Three. As leaders, we look for processes that are broken so we can fix them. Over time, we view the world as a compilation of things that are wrong, abnormal, or broken. We need to train ourselves to go into situations looking for what is going right. We need to be mindful and deliberate in these efforts, such as employing tactics like rounding with employees. And when we discover what is going right, we need to provide positive feedback.

Provide feedback in the moment.

Don't wait too long to compliment. There is no reason to hold on to positive feedback for a later time, which may never come. When the opportunity is in front of you, go for it. But, if you are reflecting on something great that happened last week that didn't get recognized, don't think that it is too late. Give that compliment today.

Be pure in your reinforcement.

Positive feedback should not be followed with "but" or "except." When delivering positive feedback as well as coaching advice, to avoid using "but" or except," you can gently move into, "You did very well in providing service recovery by getting that exam rescheduled quickly. If this were to happen again in the future, you could also consider. . ."

Compliment progress.

Don't wait for perfection before you compliment. Positive feedback is a powerful tool in improvement. Progress, not just final results, deserves positive feedback.

Know how your employees want to receive praise.

Some may enjoy being complimented in front of others. Others may cherish a handwritten note mailed to their home. There is no need to guess. Ask your employees. Also observe their responses to various types of positive feedback.

Be specific when you compliment someone.

Provide concise, positive feedback. Being too general in your positive feedback is the most common trap we fall into as we try to meet the three-to-one positivity ratio. We start doling out "atta boy," "great job," and "you're awesome," resulting in a perceived lack of sincerity and genuine appreciation. Also, a desired result of positive feedback is for desired behavior, performance, or contributions to be repeated. If the employee doesn't know specifically what they did to get an "atta boy" from the boss, they don't get the positive reinforcement that leads to performing this same way in the future.

The examples below show the contrast between general and concise feedback.

General: "Samantha, you are so good with patients. Keep up the good work."

Concise: "Samantha, I was just rounding with the inpatients today, and each one that you have cared for has mentioned you by name as going above and beyond for them. Mr. Smith mentioned that you took extra time to explain to him all of his new medications in a way that made him truly less confused about them. And, Mrs. Jones mentioned that you helped her meet her pain goal today by discussing some different options with her physician. Thank you for taking excellent care of your patients."

A leader who attended one of our public trainings reported that she was one of those leaders who struggled to provide enough sincere, concise positive feedback to her employees or peers. She chose this as a place to start in improving her leadership. She reported to us that not too long into her efforts, one of her model employees was moved to tears. The employee said to this leader, "I didn't think you even noticed me before or that you felt that way about my work." This employee had worked for this leader for years without positive feedback. Don't leave your high-performing employees to feel unnoticed when providing frequent and specific positive feedback is so easy to do. Your high-performing employees are the ones being sought out by other employers.

62   Direct Dialogue: Coaching

Everyone has opportunities to continue to grow and develop. And, given the variation in the levels of behavior, performance, and contributions, the opportunities are plentiful for you to coach and keep coaching.

In thinking about coaching conversations, you may start getting some of those feelings associated with uncomfortable or difficult conversations. Hold the phone. We want to show you how you can provide coaching feedback that resides on the positive side of the three-to-one ratio. In essence, go into each coaching conversation with the goal of making it a positive conversation.

A coaching conversation is your leadership tool for developing employees. Coaching conversations show your commitment to engage individuals to increase clarity, improve understanding, and provide impetus for change resulting in professional development, advancement of projects, and accelerated results. Coaching conversations, as described below, are very useful when coaching new employees, or employees in new roles. Even your most tenured employees may need coaching for episodic, isolated behavior or performance issues.

Coaching conversations likely won't be the right type of conversation to address behavior or performance that is chronic, persistent, and has a heavy negative impact on operations. So, knowing your employee and the details of the behavior or performance issue are important in deciding what conversation to have. If you read through the information on positive coaching conversations and your gut tells you that this approach isn't going to get you the desired results due to the severity and chronic nature of the issue, then you likely need to engage in a different type of conversation, a corrective conversation, which is described later in this solution.

For a positive coaching conversation, we recommend a commonly used "sandwich" approach in which the coaching opportunity is explored in the middle of the conversation. The outline of the conversation looks like this: Build Up-Coach Up-Support Up.

Build Up.

Thank them for what they do well. Share positive qualities and the strengths they bring to the team. Much like complimentary conversations, this feedback needs to be concise. It is also advisable to compliment the employee regarding their specific strengths that will be most helpful as he or she goes about mastering this specific coaching need that is being discussed.

Coach Up.

Cover one or two professional development opportunities. Reassure the employee that you care enough to support them in their future development. To keep coaching conversations positive, avoid "kitchen sinking" the coaching opportunities. Bringing up too many development needs in one conversation will likely turn this conversation into a negative for the employee. Prioritize one or two specific coaching topics for each coaching conversation. It's not that you are ignoring those other coaching needs; they are simply best left to future conversations. Consider a plan for a series of developmental coaching conversations if there are a lot of coaching needs. Coaching also stays positive when you engage the employee in creating the plan for success. Create this with them, don't give it to them.

Support Up.

Communicate your confidence that they can succeed. A coaching conversation stays positive and the relationship strengthens when you end this conversation with a statement such as: "I believe in you, and I am confident that you will succeed in developing your skill in this area." Offering your commitment to helping them is another positive in the closing of this conversation.

Jane and I work with leaders to practice the skill of having positive coaching conversations. Some common feedback we hear when role-playing these conversations using the Build Up-Coach Up-Support Up outline is that it feels like there is a "speed bump" when moving from the initial Build Up part of the conversation into the coaching segment. To help make the conversation flow best, and avoid any uncomfortableness with transitioning from Build Up to Coach Up, it is recommended that the leader open the conversation by stating the purpose of the conversation and the outline.

This opening could go something like: "It is great to have time with you today, Sarah, to have a conversation related to your ongoing growth and development as a housekeeper in the environmental services department. In today's conversation I want to start by providing feedback regarding what is going well, then create a plan for the ongoing development of your skills regarding the new office building cleaning tasks, and end with a joint commitment in regard to your success."

A frequently asked question by leaders is in regard to employees who have multiple coaching and development needs. Should you engage employees in selecting which coaching needs are worked on next? Our guidance in this regard is to strive to determine if there is a clear and convincing priority. If there is, go with this as the topic of your coaching conversation. Then, engage the employee in creating the improvement plan. If there are two or three coaching needs that are of equal priority, letting the employee select where to start and then jointly developing the plan is a good idea.

An example in which it was important for me to select the priority coaching need involved a new leader I was supervising and mentoring. This nurse had a career goal of being a leader. After many attempts at applying for an entry-level supervisory position, he eventually landed a night shift weekend supervision position. He had been at the organization for many years in a staff nurse role and was clinically very competent. Yet, as a new leader, he had many priority development needs.

He was also challenged in this new role, as he had been his whole life, with a severe form of dyslexia. He had learned to adapt and excel academically and clinically, yet he was struggling to adapt to the paperwork and reporting requirements of his new leadership role. Often, when discussing his transition to his new role, this was his primary focus and concern. However, as his leader, I had identified that a much greater need was his ability to transition from an employee to a leader; specifically, his ability to uphold the hospital's high standards for behavior and performance on the night shift. Trends were emerging regarding high levels of disregard for work rules (e.g., breaks, smoke-free campus, meal breaks) and behavior standards on the weekend night shifts.

If I had left the prioritization of coaching needs to this new supervisor, he would have quickly chosen the improvement of his paperwork and reporting. Yet, the priority need of the organization was for him to develop his supervisory skills to lead a high-performing team.

Follow Up to Coaching Conversations.

In many situations, coaching involves more than one conversation between a leader and an employee. Keep a nicely organized cadence of documentation and conversations to move the progress along. Establishing an appropriate frequency of check-ins with the employee shows your continued interest and support of their efforts.

A great tip that has helped many leaders in follow-up to their coaching efforts is to ask the employee to keep a formal document or log of the coaching plan and their efforts. A wise mentor once advised, "leaders don't have to do all the heavy lifting, it's the employee's success plan: let them document it and update you on their progress."

Direct Dialogue: Correcting

Positive coaching isn't always going to garner you the level of change or correction needed. Coaching doesn't work in all situations. Therefore, we need a different conversation in our leadership conversation tool-kit.

It is easy to comprehend that simply stating "your attitude is poor" or "your performance is slipping" is likely not going to be effective at improving attitude or performance. You may want corrective conversations to be short, but not at the expense of not getting the desired result from the conversation. So, you don't have to go on and on, yet you do need to prepare for and deliver a concise conversation. There are some critical elements in the conversation when something a bit stronger than a positive coaching conversation is warranted.

As was mentioned earlier, to do this right we need to prepare. Below are suggestions for preparing for those conversations that are needed when an employee is not effectively performing or complying with standards and positive coaching hasn't resulted in change.

Understand the problem.

To be prepared for direct dialogue that is corrective, you must be armed with the details of the problem, the seriousness of the impact, and an understanding of the chronic/persistent versus episodic/isolated nature of the problem. You may want to keep the conversations that seek understanding of the problem separate from the conversations that are focused on correcting the problem.

Understand and consider the overall performance level of the employee.

For the same act of noncompliance, the conversation may be different based on the historical performance level of the individual and/or the chronic versus episodic nature of the problem. For instance, two employees are tardy on two occasions this week. One employee is a high-performing employee on your team who has never been tardy in the past. The other employee is in the progressive disciplinary process for chronic tardiness. The leader needs to have a feedback conversation with each of these employees, yet these conversations will differ.

Draft the conversation.

Determine the appropriate content of conversation using some, or all, of the points from the suggested Five-Point Corrective Conversation Outline below.

The Five-Point Corrective Conversation Outline

1. Directly and concisely state what is being observed.

2. State, in detail, the impact of the behavior/performance.

3. State specific standards/expectations.

4. Describe the terms of follow-up monitoring/evaluation.

5. State specifically the consequences for lack of improvement.

The Five-Point Corrective Conversation Outline can be used in total or in part. The level of seriousness of the conversation can be lightened or intensified by the tone of voice and body language. Additionally, the conversation may be formalized as a written work plan and may include disciplinary action.

We'll explore each part of this five-point conversation, starting with the first point: "Directly and concisely state what is being observed." What are they doing or not doing? Go beyond "You are often late for work," and get specific with "Over the last four weeks, you've been tardy by five or more minutes a total of six times." You can even show them the attendance report documenting the details.

Having documentation to support what you observe is helpful in describing the problem that needs to be addressed. For instance, if a hospital registration clerk must, 100 percent of the time, scan the patient's insurance card and driver's license, you could show a report detailing the specific deficiency (e.g., 82 percent versus the required 100 percent).

But what do you do if it is behavior you have to address in this conversation? Often, it is. And often you didn't witness the behavior, as we know what happens to employee behavior when the leader enters the room—it gets better. I've adopted a phrase that I use for this point in the conversation when unobserved behavior is being addressed: *"I've heard it enough to believe that it's true."* Then I go on to detail the behaviors that are at issue.

The second point in the conversation to address is the impact of the behavior or performance. What is the affect on others, the department, and the organization? In the case of tardiness, paint the picture in detail. "When you are late for work, the first patient of the day, and each patient thereafter, is made to wait for their scheduled appointment time. The day doesn't end on time, causing several employees to receive overtime pay. We have received patient complaints to the severity of some patients wanting to no longer receive services here." This element of the conversation is one that you rarely want to leave out. It is an eye-opener and can really create motivation and understanding for the need for change.

The middle of the conversation, the third point, is to specifically state the standards and expectations. What are they supposed to be doing? If you can show a policy, manual, or other written document that clearly details the expectation, all the better. This is where written behavior standards can come in handy as a leadership tool. It can be so helpful if you can point to a written behavior standard developed by peers and not just reference your made-up expectations of behavior.

Maybe you can even demonstrate what is expected. I recall many conversations in which the employee really benefited from discussing the clarity of the expectation. It is similar to my teenage daughter and I having two different standards related to a "clean" bedroom. When I tell her to clean her room, her definition of "clean" and mine are not the same. Discussing, in detail, the definition of a clean room is good for both of us.

In this next point of the conversation, you will want to move into describing the terms of follow-up monitoring and evaluation. In this fourth point of the conversation, you will want to add how you are going to monitor if positive change is occurring or not. In those cases where you have data, like time and attendance records or error rates, this part gets a little easier. Yet you still must be diligent in following through and conducting the monitoring. You may decide to review the attendance record each week and have a weekly check-in meeting to overview the findings. Again, you must follow through. Often what gets monitored gets improved.

This gets tricky when it comes to monitoring changes in

behavior. If you didn't witness the behavior in the first place, how are you going to know if it is improving or not? With the help of some great human resource guidance, many of the monitoring plans that I engaged in involved employee rounding. It would go something like this: "Each week, I'm going to randomly select three of your coworkers to round with. I am going to ask them these three questions about your behavior as a coworker. Each week, you and I will sit down and review the feedback that I've received."

Lastly, you should conclude the conversation by stating specifically the consequences for lack of improvement. What is going to happen if they don't meet the standards or expectations within the expected time frame? We stand by the saying, "Absent consequences, you are merely offering a suggestion." I have often found that this step in the conversation is the one that many leaders have a really tough time including. It may seem harsh or mean. But I have found that it is a fair step to include.

I've seen so many examples in which leaders have gotten to the last straw with an employee's behavior or performance problem and recommend termination. Yet, in all the preceding conversations, the employees never inferred that there would be consequences if improvement wasn't achieved, and by a specific time frame. In most organizations, the human resources experts are helpful in guiding you through the understanding of the formal disciplinary steps. Also, you may need guidance on the time frame expected for change. Behavior change is hard and often takes time. We advise that up to six months may be a reasonable time frame for an employee to work on improving behavior.

After the initial Five-Point Conversation, you will be

meeting with the employee in follow-up on a consistent basis to monitor and provide feedback on the progress toward change. During this phase, it may be appropriate to engage the employee to develop problem statements and modified action plans so that he or she develops a deeper understanding of the situation. He or she may also need to do some of the up-front heavy lifting to have a stake in the game and ownership. Those employees who have truly owned their problem and work plans and engaged their leader and peers to provide support and guidance are the ones I have known to succeed at behavior change.

In some situations, however, a very short time frame for successful change may be required. For instance, if you have a heavy machine operator who is not adhering to safety standards and may harm himself or others, you don't give him six months to comply with the standard. And the consequences may be more severe. This might be stated as such: "Any instance of further noncompliance with these safety standards will lead to immediate termination of employment."

In each of the points of the conversation, it is important to avoid generalities and be as concise and specific as possible. It is hard to have direct dialogue if you haven't mustered the will or mastered the skill of being direct. Contrast the following feedback statements:

General: "You are rude to patients. I want you to be more pleasant."

Concise: "In keeping with our customer service values, it is expected that you follow the defined communication standards with patients. I am providing you with another written copy of these standards. Based on recent feedback from patient rounds, it is evident that you are not adhering to these standards. I received feedback that you talk negatively about the organization to patients, that you carry on private conversations in public, and that you conflict with coworkers in earshot of patients. These behaviors are not acceptable. You will receive the formal corrective action of a written warning in your personnel file the next time it is confirmed that you engaged in any of these types of activities."

Worth repeating is that the Five-Point Conversation can be used in total or in part. Though it may not be the most appropriate of analogies, we liken the Five-Point Conversation to a set of golf clubs. You choose the right club for the situation. If you are "far away from the hole," you use your driver, or all five points of the conversation delivered in full seriousness, without positive feedback, and with a written work plan. If you are "close to the hole," you use your putter, which may be just the first point in the conversation. You will, with practice, become skilled at knowing what club, or points of the conversation, to use. Again, a very bad choice of analogies, but one our learners seem to grasp.

When I was a vice president of a hospital, I would often attend a brief, twice-a-day huddle that was led by a nursing supervisor. The purpose of this huddle was to assess the patient volumes, acuities, and the corresponding staffing and competencies. One day, I entered the already started huddle that was being led by a very experienced leader. I had worked with her for many years and knew her to be a stellar fiscal steward. She knew nursing, and she knew management and finance.

So it surprised me that day to observe in the huddle that

this leader carried out a decision that increased labor expenses on this shift, seemingly without justification of patient volumes or acuity. Having a long-standing relationship and respect for this leader's abilities to manage finances well, I pulled out the putter. After the huddle, in a private conversation, I simply stated what I observed. "I heard you report the staffing plan during the huddle. The staffing you reported for the medical unit was one team in excess of the defined staffing plan."

Then I listened. That was all it took for her to engage in a conversation about personal issues that were carrying over into the workplace. In short, she admitted to "giving in" to employees who wanted an extra team to make the patient care assignments a bit lighter on this given day.

I didn't need to get into the points two through five of the Five-Point Conversation. It wasn't necessary knowing what I knew about this employee. She knew the impact, she knew what was expected, and I didn't need to lay out a monitoring plan or consequences. If I had chosen to do so, I could have damaged our relationship with no added benefit in changing her performance. Stating what I observed was enough.

Then, of course, there are situations when, indeed, you will need to use several of the conversation points. Or, in those times of severe issues of behavior or performance where you have your highest need of change, you will need all five points. You will need your driver.

As part of the preparation for these constructive conversations, you need to prepare for the types of reactions that may occur. You may have this wonderfully prepared Five-Point Conversation, yet not be able to communicate those points given the reaction of the employee. The main response to any reaction is to gain control of the conversation and get it back on track to the points you have prepared to make in the conversation. There are going to be attempts to derail the conversation. They come in many forms. When you think you've seen it all, you'll experience a new reaction.

To assist with preparation, you may want to consider how you would respond to the following statements:

1. "When was the last time you walked in our shoes? You have no clue what is really going on around here. We are short-staffed and overworked. If our customers aren't happy, it's management's fault, not mine."

2. "Who told you this bunch of crap? I have a right to know."

3. "So I make mistakes once in a while. So do you. You want me to list them all for you?"

4. "I'm not going to sit here and take this nonsense from you." (Employee gets up to leave.)

5. Employee cries. "You are right. I'm stupid. I should just quit."

6. "I'm not going to take this from you or anybody! This is harassment." (Employee's behavior becomes physically threatening.)

7. "You've never liked me. This is so unfair."

8. "Everyone else does this too. Why are you only picking on me?"

While the most powerful conversations are face-to-face, following up in writing is certainly advisable. I have sent many emails beginning with: "Per our conversation today. . ." Recounting the conversation, in writing, as a record that you and the employee can reference in the future can be helpful for both parties. You will want to end these follow-up written communications with a request that the employee respond if any of the summarized information doesn't accurately reflect their recollection of the conversation or if further clarification of the information is needed. My experience is that the human resource professionals appreciate a leader who keeps such written records.

Beyond the need to provide feedback to individuals, there will be times when you may want to provide performance feedback to an entire group or department of employees all at once. This might be in the form of an employee meeting, posting, or email. We caution against the use of group feedback when there is a high likelihood that the feedback truly just needs to reach a few members of your team. We may run into this trap of thinking that this is an efficient way to address problems; however, it is not an effective way.

For instance, a mass email that goes out to all of the surgery employees that reads something like this:

> *We have a recent trend of surgical specimens that are not labeled correctly. The policy is attached. Please re-read the policy. Consider this a reminder. Further incidences of non-compliance will be subject to discipline.*

I know that the leader of this department has access to information that will identify the specific specimen-labeling errors and the individuals who were responsible for the labeling. So why the email to all? It is easy. It is quick. It is less uncomfortable. But oh, it is not good for employee morale. The people who the message is intended for may not think it applies to them, so they disregard it, or maybe they won't even read it. Your highest performing employees, who this message doesn't apply to, are often offended.

When you feel the urge to do this, usually it is out of a sense of urgency and a desire to act quickly. This is when you should pause and reflect on not only the most efficient way to provide this feedback, but also on the most effective way to do so. Reflect on whether you are attempting to use group communication to address specific performance issues that likely belong to a few individuals. Group communication is rarely effective at getting to the individual issues.

We find so many examples of this in workplaces that we assess. We encounter many employees who are dissatisfied and leaders who are pondering why issues haven't improved in follow-up to this type of feedback.

I recall a situation in which a large medical staff, which had been proud of award-winning patient care, started to notice some quality results that were trending downward. They may have panicked, because their response was to schedule mandatory retraining for all physicians on the care of a certain type of patient. Thank goodness, prior to this big investment of time in training, the extra effort was taken to evaluate the quality data further. The data was able to point to two physicians, not all, who would benefit from a face-to-face conversation in regard to the findings. As you can imagine, this was much more effective in the resolution of the problem.

So, avoid "painting everyone with the same brush" in relation to performance feedback for noncompliance. Take the time to investigate and determine who you need to have a face-to-face conversation with. Then, determine which points of the Five-Point Conversation are needed to get the best response and result.

Employee-to-Employee Performance Feedback

Performance feedback doesn't always have to come from leaders. In high-performing organizations, there is a higher prevalence of employee-to-employee feedback regarding behavior and performance. High-performing organizations often have a culture in which employees are able, and willing, to call each other out.

Solve problems at the lowest possible level, with the least amount of bureaucracy and paperwork.

Help employees to be able to solve their own work and/or interpersonal conflicts in a tactful, constructive, and professional manner. More precisely, in a manner that builds relationships with their peers. Encourage them. Role model it for them. Help them to prepare.

In my earlier days of leadership, my manner of dealing with employee-to-employee work issues was much different and definitely less effective. If an employee came to me with a complaint about a coworker, I would go to the coworker and get their side of the story, and then back and forth I would go as the go-between in trying to solve their issue. This was a foolish waste of time. Contrast that to the Stan and Joe story below.

On this given day, I started my morning by reviewing my emails. In doing so, I happened across an email from Joe. Joe was an evening housekeeper in the hospital in which I was a vice president. His boss was on vacation, so he went up the chain of command to me, with an emailed complaint about his coworker Stan. His email, typed in all capital letters with many exclamation points, relayed his strong allegation about his coworker having been caught looking in Joe's employee locker. He alleged that he was sure Stan stole something from him, yet he didn't know what. He went on to say that he would never trust Stan again and never wanted to work on the same shift with him again. He insisted that I do something about it, NOW!

In my newfound way of dealing with coworker complaints, this is what I did: I waited for Joe to come to work that afternoon. I sought him out. I inquired of him, "Joe, you have to tell me the rest of the story. What did you say to Stan when you caught him in your employee locker last night?"

Joe's response was that he had not confronted Stan when he witnessed him in his locker. Joe responded that he went straight to the computer and typed the email to me. Joe stated that it was my job to deal with it, not his. This is the point where we can turn it around as leaders. Joe is an adult. No one, I assume, takes care of these types of issues for him outside of work, so why is it necessary for others to address his issues at work?

This is where the conversation turned to me coaching Joe. We spent a short amount of time preparing him for the conversation he was going to have with Stan, not the conversation I was going to have with Stan.

Joe went to Stan and stated what he observed. "Stan, I saw you going into my locker last night."

Stan's sincere response to Joe was, "Hey, bud, I thought I had worn my coat in to work last night and when I went to go outside on my break, my coat wasn't in my locker so I thought maybe I had accidently put it in your locker since it is right next to mine."

It was the truth, and Joe believed it. If I had talked to Stan and delivered the response to Joe, do you think he would have believed it? Not likely. The conversation and the important nonverbal communication helped Joe to believe what Stan was telling him.

We rob our employees of the ability to strengthen and rebuild relationships when we become the go-between. Don't limit the development of your employees. Coach and empower them to become better.

Call to Action

The most powerful conversations are one-on-one, face-to-face. Many before us have suggested that "the conversation is the relationship." One conversation at a time you are maintaining, building, diminishing, or destroying your relationship. Conversations are important to your leadership. Conversations are important to the quality of the employee experience.

Providing performance feedback in the form of dialogue is an important part of any leader's job. Mustering the will and mastering the skill of direct dialogue will serve your leadership well. The following Success Plan can provide you with guidance in this regard.

Performance Feedback Success Plan

Evaluate Current State

- Evaluate trends in recent years related to employee satisfaction or engagement survey data and comments in regard to perceptions of leadership feedback and/or performance management.

- Evaluate turnover of employees in past two years. Evaluate for "good turnover" (loss of low-behaving/performing employees) versus "bad turnover" (loss of employees who meet or exceed behavior and performance standards).

- Seek understanding of current organizational standards for employee behavior, performance, and contributions.

- Seek understanding of current disciplinary process.

- Consider who are the communication experts around you who could possibly serve as a mentor.

Plan and Make Improvements—
Select and Prioritize Based on Assessment

- Create a systematic practice of providing employee feedback (one-on-one, face-to-face).

- Evaluate all future employee satisfaction or engagement survey data and comments in regard to perceptions of leadership feedback and/or performance management.

- Seek out opportunities daily to provide feedback on behavior, performance, and contributions. Prepare well for the challenging ones.

- Engage a mentor to assist in preparing for and evaluating your performance feedback conversations.

Evaluate and Adjust

- Regularly reassess to evaluate if the changes are leading to improvements. Adjust plan and improvement activities as necessary. Solution Twelve can guide you.

Recognition, Celebration, and Appreciation

When Sue and I step into one of our partner healthcare organizations and proceed to explain to every leader who works there how imperative it is that they develop a cadence of recognition, celebration, and appreciation, there are some faces in the room that are acutely turned off. In fact, in some audiences, you can hear the proverbial pin drop.

Saying thanks and showing gratitude may be considered "fluff" by some members of your organization (or you) and not deemed a "true" leadership skill.

It is a leadership skill and a very important one. Unfortunately, not everyone was born with this natural belief or ability, nor was everyone raised in a household that demonstrated appreciation and gratitude.

Think about recognition, celebration, and appreciation in the same way as other leadership skills. Although some people do not easily grasp the concepts of budgeting and income state-ments, they are still expected to develop these skills as a leader. The same goes for celebrating progress or accomplishment, rec-ognizing a job well done, and demonstrating appreciation.

At times, Sue and I hear excuses from leaders as to why they cannot recognize or show appreciation to their employees more often. Some of those excuses are:

"Employees will think I am being fake or insincere."

"I don't understand why I have to thank them for just doing their jobs."

"I buy them pizza all the time. Isn't that thanks enough?"

"Nobody is thanking me for the job I do every day."

"They will think I am playing favorites if I recognize one person over another."

All are untrue. I feel sorry for those who never receive thanks or appreciation for their efforts. I truly do. The buck stops here. It is never too late, and it is free for you to provide appreci-ation and recognition for your employees in some fashion, daily.

The great news is that even if you are not an especially positive or thankful person who sees opportunities to express gratitude every day, you can develop this skill. I will expand on how to do that later in this solution.

The benefits of expressing thanks and gratitude are plen-tiful. Employees often leave their leaders and their jobs because they feel unappreciated. Yet we can easily counter those feelings by creating simple new habits.

Another upside to recognizing amazing employee behav-ior and performance is that what gets recognized, gets repeated.

Behaviors and performance that get recognized, get repeated!

Appreciation also affects engagement. Engagement affects profit margins and lower voluntary turnover. According to Towers Watson, a 15 percent higher employee engagement correlates with a 2 percent uptick in profit margins. Gallup states that those businesses in the top quartile of engagement scores average 22 percent higher profitability. Globoforce reports that employers with effective recognition initiatives have a 31 percent lower voluntary turnover rate.

Showing recognition and appreciation increases productivity. Employees who *are recognized* for meeting a goal or a job well done for something *specific* are 23 percent more productive at work. Workers who feel *cared for* or work in an environment where they know others *show care and concern* for them as people are 43 percent more productive at work.

**Recognition (for something specific)
and appreciation (care and concern about the person)
can increase productivity.**

And that's not all. Gratitude improves you as a person and a leader. It is a skill to be developed that will help you at home and at work. Gratitude opens up the brain for critical thinking to occur and creates more positivity in you. It benefits the giver and the receiver.

You and the people around you deserve this positivity. Some need it more than others. Even your lowest-performing and worst-behaving employees do many things right; you want them to change in a positive way. Likely you've experienced that behavior change is difficult, and celebrating behaviors and performance that you want to see repeated will be of help.

Let's differentiate between recognition and appreciation for a moment. Mike Robbins, author of *Focus on the Good Stuff*, makes the distinction between the two. I believe that it is a distinction that all leaders need to contemplate. We encourage you to recognize what you want to see more of. We promote that you celebrate goal achievement loudly and often. However, both celebration and recognition are finite and usually come from leaders to employees. They are given in relationship to an event or attainment of an objective or goal. You may recognize someone for a job well done with a project or succeeding on a particularly brutal day. Recognition goes away when the goal is met or the achievement is passed. You indeed need to recognize and celebrate, yet you also need to *appreciate*.

Appreciation is different. You aren't recognizing employees based on an event, you are appreciating peers or employees just for who they are. You are showing gratitude for their personality, their work ethic, and their humanness. These are key things to appreciate because they *always* happen. It is their genetic make-up and the goodness you likely saw when you hired them and now as you lead them.

Robbins, a former baseball pitcher, makes the point that you *celebrate* a win. As a pitcher, you get *recognized* for pitching a no-hitter. Yet, when the team loses, or when the pitcher gets pulled from the game in the second inning because he's given up a lot of runs, he still needs to feel appreciated, to feel cared for.

When you consider that many employees leave their jobs because they feel underappreciated, focusing on appreciation and gratitude is a key leadership skill for you to hone in on. Think of all that your employees do that is not tied to one specific achievement. It is not tied to longevity of service. People shouldn't wait for recognition every five years at a longevity award ceremony! Yes, service award and longevity ceremonies are very nice gestures. You want your rock stars to stay with you and to celebrate the fact they are remaining at work with you. This just cannot be the only appreciation your employees receive.

Recognize: to acknowledge or take notice of in some definite way.

Appreciate: to understand the worth or importance of (something or someone); to admire and value (something or someone).

Celebrate: to do something special or enjoyable for an important event, occasion, holiday, etc.; to praise (someone or something); to say that (someone or something) is great or important.

Gratitude: the state of being grateful; thankfulness.

Source: *Merriam-Webster's Dictionary*

Positivity

Barbara Frederickson's book, *Positivity*, includes my absolute favorite quote: "Negativity screams at you, and positivity only whispers." Indeed, we hear negativity screaming at us often, and therefore we cannot overcompliment others enough to drown it out on many days.

Leaders will admit to me that they are afraid of overappreciating their employees and being thought of as a fake. Frederickson reminds us that none of us likely have enough time to overappreciate. The ratio of "too much appreciation" is seventeen compliments to every one criticism or critique. With all that leaders have on their plates, there are likely no worries of overappreciating employees.

You can, however, create an effective work environment where employees feel appreciated. Frederickson advises that a healthy ratio of compliments to criticism or critique is three-to-one. If you lead a work environment that is currently experiencing a ratio of two-to-one, or even one-to-one, it has a negative impact on employee satisfaction and engagement, teamwork, achievement, and productivity.

This does not mean that you need to run to your computer, create a spreadsheet, and make a hash mark in it every time you provide appreciation or thank an employee. Just knowing that you should strive for a ratio of at least three-to-one will push you to step it up.

To recognize and appreciate the positive things going on around you, first you have to see them or learn about them.

Rounding with your employees does provide an opportunity to hear about it. And one simple tactic that Sue and I know that works for seeing it is: *get out of your office*. It is difficult to find positivity from your desk. In order to see all of the great things happening in your department or organization, you need to be present and see them happening. Go out and find the positive that whispers. It is likely right outside your door.

Three Good Things

Leading with positivity takes practice. Our brains are simply not trained to look for positives. Add a busy day in leadership, which includes those around you throwing all the bad stuff your way, and you may feel like a salmon swimming upstream to find one thing that is positive.

Yes, there are days like that. However, you can train your brain to think positively and to seek out the good things. Knowing that gratitude, appreciation, and recognition are going to have a positive and immediate effect on employees should motivate you to look for the positive.

Before I learned about "Three Good Things," I simply just set a challenge for myself that I would daily either publicly appreciate someone or write them a thank-you note. This deliberate attempt required me to search for one good thing in my work environment. I found myself saying, "Oh, that one thing wasn't really good enough. I better keep looking." Or, "It's two o'clock in the afternoon, and I have not found anyone to thank today. I better keep looking."

When I started this practice, I had just lost fourteen

employees in a very short span of time to competing employers in the region. It was devastating to me, and I had gotten super whiny about it. When I learned about the power of expressing appreciation and gratitude, I felt very guilty that I had not been appreciating the employees that had not left. These employees had the same opportunities to leave; yet I had more than forty employees who stayed.

I immediately challenged myself to thank them every day somehow, and the results were amazing. With lightning speed, a team of survivors was built. It took nearly six months to replace all those who had left and to rebuild my team, but it was stronger than ever.

Now that I knew the power of appreciation and gratitude and what it was doing for me as well as others, I needed to step up my practice.

Erika Oliver, author of the book *Three Good Things*, shares her personal story of how the daily practice of uncovering and sharing three good things changed her marriage and her life. And what I have experienced while documenting three good things on a daily basis is an improvement in my professional and personal life.

On a more researched level, the value of acknowledging three good things at the end of each day is being studied by the Duke Patient Safety Center. In this study, cohort participants are prompted to write down three positive occurrences in their life every day for two weeks. Dr. Bryan Sexton from the center reports that after less than a week, participants start thinking about positive occurrences throughout the day. Some 98 percent of participants in one cohort completed this exercise of documenting three good things in just three minutes per day, yet it is estimated that participating has twice the efficacy of Prozac on the brain, Sexton said.

The concept is researched, yet amazingly simple. Each day, think of three good things that happened. State them out loud or write them down at the end of the day. Pretty soon, events that you may have glossed over become a positive force in your day.

The bottom line is that in order to appreciate and recognize others, you need to open up your brain to notice when great things are happening that may not be mind-blowing or obvious but deserve appreciation and recognition all the same.

Hormones

What do hormones have to do with it? As if you didn't have enough going against you as your brain struggles to seek out positivity, you are also affected by hormones.

It is well known that the hormone cortisol is secreted during stressful times, creating a "fight or flight" response. Cortisol has often been referred to as the "stress hormone."

Negativity in the workplace can have the effect of cortisol secretion. When negative or disturbing events happen, cortisol is released and then lasts twenty-six hours in the body.

When you have a negative or bothersome conversation, what if you ruminate on it a bit? We all know some people who worry about a negative comment made to them for days or longer. As leaders, this puts us even more on stage and in the hot seat for careless conversations.

I once made a sarcastic comment to one of my very valuable employees. He was a preceptor on the night shift for many of our department's new nurses. He requested an extension of the orientation period of a new nurse, and I personally felt that she was ready to complete her orientation. I denied the extension, and I used sarcastic humor to gloss over the fact I was not giving him what he asked for.

Prior to this, this preceptor would converse with me on at least a weekly basis. This stopped with my hurtful comments. After three months of this preceptor not speaking to me, I finally sought him out. He relayed that he was still angry with me for making those sarcastic comments to him. Of course, I apologized and we worked it out, yet think of the cortisol pumping through his body—possibly for months! Think of the negative thoughts he likely had about his leader and employer. Imagine how this may have affected his attitude and work performance.

Another hormone, oxytocin, is released when there is positivity. Oxytocin is referred to as the "love hormone" and reacts in the body as the very opposite of cortisol. Praise, gratitude, appreciation, positive thoughts, a positive event in the day, or a welcomed physical touch will all cause the body to release oxytocin.

The human brain "lights up" on an MRI when oxytocin is released. The parts of the brain that are stimulated by this hormone positively affect communication, collaboration, and critical thinking. I like to refer to this as the "3 Cs."

However, very unlike cortisol, the hormone oxytocin quickly dissipates in the bloodstream.

Remember the three-to-one ratio for creating a positive

work environment? Positivity needs to be present at a three-to-one ratio or greater to counter the cortisol that is hanging out so long in our bodies in response to each incident of negativity or perceived negativity. The three-to-one ratio will help to ensure that you and your employees are creating a work environment where the "3 Cs" can happen.

The Power of a SIMPLE Note

Once I started the simple practice of writing thank-you notes, I soon knew that I would never give it up. It is so powerful. Sue and I have multiple stories of "thank you for the thank-you note." A common response from an employee who received a thank-you note was along the lines of, "You know, I had forgotten about that family I helped (or whatever event was recognized), so when I got your thank-you note at home in the mail, I re-lived it all over again. It felt great. I really needed that today. You have no idea."

When you write a thank-you note to show appreciation and recognition for the actions and behaviors of an individual, you are showering them with positive thoughts (and oxytocin), which recycles an event that already happened.

Many of the tactics that we recommend in this book take time to implement and then time to see the results. You must stay the course and be diligent to not give up before forming the new habit and experiencing the positive results. This practice of writing thank-you notes, with your own style, in your handwriting, and mailing to your employees' homes is an overnight smash success! It positively impacts the life of that one individual, who then comes to work and creates a ripple effect of positivity. Each and every thank-you note has power beyond belief. It is truly the "pixie dust" of leadership, and there is no reason to not "just start!"

> *Dear Julie,*
>
> *I wanted to drop you a line and let you know how very much you are appreciated for your work in the role of Employee Relations Manager. It goes far beyond your organizational skills and the efficiency with which you perform your work. It is the obvious belief that you have in creating a great work environment for our employees. An example is seeing you at the holiday meet-and-greet with Santa and Mrs. Claus for our employees and their children. It is so important for our employees to see each other beyond the workplace, and you have created an event where everyone is beaming, and it has nothing to do with Santa Claus!*
>
> *Susan let me know that, as your leader, she is so appreciative of your skills as well. More than that, she stated to me that you are a team member who can be counted on in every situation.*
>
> *Thank you for the work you do every day. You likely do not hear enough what a difference you make in the lives of all 900 employees and their families.*
>
> *Jane*

We advocate sending thank-you notes to the employee's home for a couple of reasons. Employees can open the note at their leisure and really feel the positive effect. Thank-you notes received at home are often viewed by family members. These are the same family members that are missing their mom, dad, husband, wife, or significant other daily.

These family members may often only hear that things are bad at the office, so wouldn't it be nice for them to hear about the positives of their loved one? The positivity is then spread to them as well!

Another great reason to send these notes to the employee's home is that some people are very private about receiving recognition. While they deserve (and likely desire) recognition, some employees may not want this to be a public display.

If you have not written a thank-you note in a while (or ever!), please know that sincerity and simplicity are recommended. Sue and I worked with a social worker named Marie who we both admired very much. Marie was a little critical of the recognition process of writing thank-you notes when this tactic was first adopted by the hospital where we worked together. She had a desire to make sure all employees were thanked equally. Choosing one person a day to thank rankled her "all things created equal" internal mechanism. Yet, soon after she experienced the magic of affecting employees profoundly with a thank-you note sent to their home, she became our organization's internal champion. She volunteered to train all new leaders on the power of thank-you notes and created an acronym for this teaching called "SIMPLE." Marie has since passed away, and she is deeply missed. We honor her memory and her work through sharing this with others.

Writing a Thank-You Note is S.I.M.P.L.E.

■ **S**incere. The note does not need to be "mushy," but it must be real!

■ **I**nclude the behavior you are recognizing (and want repeated!). Be specific.

■ **M**ention others in a positive light ("manage them up") when you can.

■ **P**ersonalize to your own style, and handwrite the thank-you note.

■ **L**eave some white space. You do not need to fill the whole card.

■ **E**nvelop the process into your weekly routine. Create a cadence of accountability for thank-you notes!

While teaching at one of our public training Summits, an attendee shared his story of how the habit of writing thank-you notes has affected him. He had started this new practice over the past months. There was a large group of employees that he had wanted to recognize for quite some time, and the task seemed daunting. So, he simply started by writing one or two thank-you notes at the start of each day. What he discovered was this new daily habit was changing each of his days into positive days. By starting his day with the act of showing appreciation, he was becoming more positive. Having been a leader for decades, he felt renewed in his leadership.

He emphasized an important point. Recognition is good for the giver and the receiver.

Beyond a Thank-You Note

As you begin your habit of rounding daily while you work and intentionally seeking out positivity, you will start to uncover all the amazing things happening around you. At some point you may wonder, "What am I going to do with all of the opportunities for recognition, appreciation, and celebration that I am gathering?"

I got this way in my leadership practice. I was writing twenty or more thank-you notes a week and could have written more. So, I decided to carry out recognition and appreciation in different ways. I realized that there were some people (mostly from the millennial generation!) who appreciated a text that might have looked something like this: "Great job on your quality audits last night!"

There were groups of employees who might have gotten an email something like this: "The patients I spoke with this morning were raving about bedside shift report. Great job with this new report process!"

If I heard something amazing about an employee who was working that day, I would seek them out and tell them what I had heard. "I just spoke to the family of your patient in room 118. They let me know how well you are managing their mother's pain. Thank you for your care and diligence. You are a great nurse. I appreciate you."

I then started bringing recognition into every staff meeting, project meeting, or huddle. It became the first agenda item at these gatherings. Do not be hesitant to do this. Recognize publicly those employees who have taken action to contribute to the progress or results. "Everyone does a great job" is watered-down praise and will not have the same effect. Be positive, yet be specific about what's great. Starting a meeting on a positive note can also stimulate the "3 Cs": collaboration, communication, and critical thinking. What a great way to start a productive meeting.

Another way to make employee recognition fun, convenient, and easy is to create a well-stocked recognition toolkit. The purpose is to have recognition items right at your fingertips to make recognition easy and timely. This toolkit doesn't have to be elaborate or expensive—it must be heartfelt and sincere, even if it is fun.

In an organization where I worked, the leaders gathered together to generate ideas for the contents of the recognition toolkits. Some toolkit ideas that came out of that session were:

- Scratch-off lottery cards (with a note that says: "We are lucky to have you on our team. Thanks for...").

- Candy such as Kudos, Lifesavers, Mr. Goodbar, or Starburst, coupled with a clever handwritten note.

- Blank certificates for Team Player, Complaint Resolution, Going the Extra Mile, Morale Booster, Living Our Values, Coworker Support, Good Humor, Star Performer, and many more.

- Pre-printed stickers (to wear on clothing or uniform), pre-printed Post-it notes and/or magnets (for a locker or computer).

- Trinkets with your organization's logo and thanks (e.g. stress balls, stars, badges).

To keep the toolkit in action, the team also created a process for replenishing supplies and allocating funds in a special-expense line item.

There are obviously many ways to show recognition and appreciation. But which are the right ones? This is where rounding with your employees and developing a relationship with them proves helpful. People can get dicey about recognition. I had an employee who worked for me who literally said to me, "You don't publicly recognize me often enough for everything I do." I never saw that one coming as a reason for dissatisfaction with my leadership. This employee clearly preferred to be recognized publicly. Not everyone does, but she does. I should have known that about her.

If I had asked this employee how she liked to be recognized and her reply was, "Loudly, often, and publicly," I could have gotten over my own paradigm that everyone wants humble, quiet recognition, and I could have met her need for public recognition.

There are those who enjoy some public recognition for a project that they took special pride in working on, or for their everyday work that is stellar. These employees may never ask for this recognition or appreciation, but they respond positively when it is given!

Then there are those who just do not want public recognition.

They may secretly enjoy a thank-you note sent to their home, but they may never even acknowledge that they received it.

I had a physician ask me to no longer send thank-you notes to his home. He is a very fine physician, deserving of thanks, recognition, and appreciation. I knew him very well. I had observed how he appeared uncomfortable in front of his peers when thanked publicly at a medical staff meeting. So I thought that a private note to his home would be the best way to recognize him.

Not so, as it turned out. His reasoning for not wanting any future thank-you notes was, "Give them to someone more deserving than I."

I let him know that I may recognize him in a private conversation more often, or I may occasionally pull the trigger on a thank-you note again, but I would not tell others never to write him a thank-you note. Then I encouraged him to simply say, "Thank you for the thank-you note." He said he would try.

Sometimes we need to promote that people show more appreciation, and sometimes we need to encourage the acceptance of it.

Peer Recognition and Appreciation

Recognition and appreciation don't just have to come from leaders to employees. Promoting employee-to-employee recognition will help in the efforts to create that positive working environment where employees thrive and great results are achieved. Leaders cannot be the only ones spreading this joy around!

In the healthcare organizations that we partner with, we encourage their Employee Experience Team (see Solution Six) to develop a peer recognition program. The fun and creativity are at an all-time high as the team creates the program. Their objective is for the recognition program to be designed in such a way that it makes it quick, easy, and readily available for employees to recognize someone. Often this takes the form of a thank-you note or certificate that is provided to the employee or placed on public display. There may be prize drawings or token recognition gifts involved as well.

What you want to have is oxytocin flowing from lots of recognition activities — during the day, at night, and on weekends. And not just when leaders are around.

Recognition from Customers

I found that my employees really loved reading the thank-you notes from patients or the positive comments from a patient satisfaction survey. Even if employees were not individually named in the note or survey comment, receiving this recognition from patients likely increased the employees' positivity and pride.

Include in your practice some customer-to-employee recognition. Display letters from customers on a recognition board or send out monthly emails recognizing those employees that were mentioned in a survey. Consider how this might work best in your department or organization.

Celebration

I have covered a lot on the topic of individual recognition and appreciation, yet group celebration is equally as important. And, it is fun. While likely most people will enjoy a celebration, some don't enjoy being the organizers of it. Creating celebrations may not be your thing.

But you likely know who these party organizers in your department or organization are. Find them. They are out there, always planning a potluck, and they know everyone's birthday by heart and organize the party. Give them the unofficial title of Chief Party Officer. Empower them to create fun and meaning-ful celebrations. Give them a budget. Then, set them free!

Your role then is to connect the celebration to a purpose or reason to celebrate. It is okay to very occasionally have a gen-eral "atta boys and girls" pizza day for no other reason than you feel like it and your perception is that everyone has been working hard. However, your team celebrations will go further in promoting great work and behavior when you connect the dots in your employees' minds between the celebration and the reason for it.

When I was a leader of a large inpatient nursing unit in a community hospital, my department had been working on a goal to get our response time to patients' call lights down to un-der two minutes on average. This would take a department-wide effort, and my employees were fired up and engaged.

To keep track of how we were doing, I would run reports on the response times, and I posted the number where employ-ees could see it each day. We had to be under the average of two minutes for three full months before we met our goal and could celebrate.

Over that time, I witnessed an increase in employees help-ing each other. The team had a goal, and they looked forward to celebrating their achievement. And they were making it happen.

On May 5, we reached our goal. And soon after, we celebrated with a huge Cinco de Mayo party right there in northern Michigan! It was still cold outside in our northern locale, but it was warm in our department. We decorated with a fake cactus. We took turns wearing the sombrero. We made stickers for employees, physicians, patients, and visitors to wear that day that said, "We are speedy! Ask about our response time!"

A couple of the department's chief party officers came over to my house the night before, and we cooked rice, beans, taco meat, and figured out a recipe for nonalcoholic margaritas. The next day, we had an amazing feast in our employee lounge, which was decorated in a Cinco de Mayo theme, along with big posters boasting the results of what we were celebrating. The CEO was invited to our department to congratulate the employees.

We did all of this for the cost of about a hundred dollars. Amazing. When we were taking down the décor, an employee asked me, "Can you make sure I am scheduled to work during the Cinco de Mayo celebration next year? That was fun!"

Celebrate often.
Celebrate for a reason.

There are some guidelines to consider for celebration. One is frequency, another is timing, and yet another is simplicity. Sue and I often coach our partner healthcare organizations to celebrate more often. When we learn of their amazing results or a story of great progress, we will ask, "How are you celebrating this?"

They often respond, "We *knew* you were going to ask that!"

What we don't want to hear is that they are putting together a team of twelve with a goal of planning a celebration that will occur in six weeks. No. Stop the madness. Keep it simple. Keep it timely to the achievement that you are celebrating. Keep it light. Keep it fun. You don't need to spend a lot of money!

Call to Action

First, seek out the positives. Then, recognize, celebrate, or appreciate them. In response, more great things will start to happen. This is a wonderful, continuous cycle.

Don't be seeking out only the most glorious of accomplishments or achievements to recognize. Guard against being that person who only recognizes very *obvious* results and metrics. A great mentor told me once that there are B players on every team. Not everyone can be an A player, and you need the B players just as much. You may be taking for granted those employees who also deserve recognition and appreciation.

Just start. Go find something good. Go find great, amazing people doing incredible work. Go find the positivity that is whispering. When you find them and respond with recognition, watch the positivity grow like a flower toward the sunlight.

Recognition, Celebration, and Appreciation Success Plan

Evaluate Current State

- Assessment — Review currently utilized employee survey results on a department-specific or organization-wide level. Look for survey findings regarding employees' perceptions of recognition, appreciation, and celebration in the workplace. Which findings are positive? Which findings point to opportunities for improvement?

■ Assessment—Reflect on your own leadership in regard to recognition, celebration, and appreciation. How do you recognize employees? How do you show appreciation? When was the last time a celebration was held, and what was being celebrated? How would you rate the positivity ratio in your department or organization? Review your recent written communications that provided recognition. Are they specific enough? Were they timely? Are there visible signs of recognition such as a thank-you or recognition board or a celebration banner? Round with employees and ask them how they prefer to be recognized and for their views on the current state of positivity and recognition.

■ Assessment—What organization-wide recognition programs are currently in place? Are they well utilized? How are accomplishments celebrated? When was the last time an organization-wide celebration was held, and what was being celebrated?

Plan and Make Improvements— Select and Prioritize Based on Assessment

■ Develop a goal and quarterly action plans for improving

the employee engagement results related to recognition, celebration, and appreciation. Utilize the information in this solution for action steps for your plan. This may include assigning a chief party officer and establishing a budget, purchasing thank-you notes and committing to send a certain number each week, or assembling and using a recognition toolkit.

- Develop a personal plan to improve positivity, recognition, and appreciation. Demonstrate group, personal, private, or public appreciation daily. Develop a practice of journaling three good things each day. Start each meeting and rounding session focused on positivity or recognition.

- **Organization Change Agent:** Advocate for organization-wide adoption of an employee-to-employee and/or customer-to-employee recognition program. Advocate for organization-wide celebrations of accomplishments or progress toward goals.

Evaluate and Adjust

- Develop and implement a plan for the monitoring of results of the improvement efforts through mini-surveys and/or rounding. Adjust the action plan based on this feedback.

- Regularly reassess to evaluate if the changes are leading to improvements. Adjust plan and improvement activities as necessary. Refer to Solution Twelve for additional guidance.

Hire Tough, Manage Easy

Peak nursing shortage. Vacancy rates reaching as high as forty percent in some units. Pressure from all sides to fill the open positions. I clearly recall these times. They remain etched into my memory as both times of dire need and optimal learning. Nurses were working maximum amounts of overtime and showing signs of burnout. We were doling out premium expenses for traveling nurses wherever we could, and each shift became a grand struggle to balance staffing demands for patient care with ever-mounting tension.

During times like that, it was easy to fall prey to the hiring mode of "upright and licensed is good enough." Skimping on the logical steps of a great hiring process became the new norm, leading to many wrong hiring decisions, such as the very experienced emergency room nurse that we hired (ignoring the mediocre reference check) who we quickly found out lacked basic hand-hygiene skills. Or an obstetrical nurse with twenty years experience that we paid relocation and sign-on bonuses to after only a phone interview and who ended up not even making it through her ninety-day probationary period.

Studies show that making poor hiring decisions like these can cost an organization one to five times the employee's annual salary, decrease employee morale, negatively impact client relations, and decrease sales (Schober, 2013).

Effective hiring and onboarding processes are needed at all times, especially in those moments when all seems to be chaos around us. Keeping to these processes can be our beacon on the shore during the storm. Swaying away from great selection processes can negatively affect our efforts to have a great employee experience.

Most likely, each of us vividly remembers our own past interviews and orientation experiences. These past experiences, good or bad, may have heavily influenced our opinion of a new employer. Perhaps these events even set the foundation for our loyalty to the organization.

Whether hiring in peak growth or crisis vacancy times, or in the midst of normal day-to-day hiring efforts, we want to create hiring and onboarding practices that provide rock-solid first impressions to our new hires, laying down roots that will blossom into excellent employees. We want to engage our employees immediately, letting nary a doubt slip into their minds when they reflect on their new employment. This solution is chock-full of high-performance practices that will help you to do just that.

The "Hiring Right" Process

The Applicant Pool

In the most perfect of worlds, every batch of new candidates will be massive, and you will have sufficient time and data to make an informed decision. Unfortunately, this isn't always the case. In those situations where you have a small spattering of possible future employees, it can be easy to simply "pick the best of the few," when the reality of the situation may be that none of them is the correct fit. Sure, it can seem a tad overwhelming to have a vast applicant pool staring back at you. Yet a large applicant pool is the ideal, providing a greater opportunity to find just the right fit for the organization.

I have sat facing that vast applicant pool many times in my career. There was one time we were searching for a new director of human resources, and the pool was far larger than we had expected, topping nearly one hundred applicants. In a meeting with the selection panel, I remember placing my hand on top of the huge pile of applications, looking out to them, and saying, "Our pearl is in here. Our job is to find him or her."

And find her we did. In the unlikeliest of places. She was living in Japan at the time, looking to relocate back to the United States as her husband was retiring from military service. We had found our pearl despite the amount of water we needed to tread to get to her. We put the work in.

Some of you may be asking, "How do I increase my applicant pool?" Simply put: create a sterling reputation. Make your organization difficult to resist. High-performing applicants tend to gravitate toward high-performing organizations. They will turn down job opportunities close to home, and even those offering better compensation packages, to work for an organization they see doing great things.

Not all organizations have reached that peak level of an employee experience yet. What better time to start? Until then, when faced with a smaller than expected application pool, take care in making that final decision. Despite the pressure to fill a position, if the right candidate isn't present in the current pool, don't feel pressured to select "the best of the worst." Keep searching.

If you choose to gamble on a less than optimal hire, you will have to lead them, your team will have to work with them, and the face of your organization will have to deal with them. It's not worth it. When you settle, you sacrifice.

Preparing for the Hiring Right Process

Charles Coonradt, author of *The Better People Leader*, states that our selection mind set should be on "hiring better than you, and better than you have." Jane and I could not agree more. When striving to be a great organization, you must be willing to raise the bar on the talent and attitudes you bring in.

When doing this, consider the following:

- Who are your employees who bring their best to work each day? Who are those employees who tend to make your organization better when they are present? Who are those employees that naturally strive to go above and beyond? In essence, who are the rock stars under your employ?

■ Now, focus on the attributes of these rock stars. This list is now the hiring criteria.

As an exercise to focus on these attributes, write up a job advertisement that doesn't include a required educational degree, skill set, or credentials. Focus this job advertisement only on the behaviors, attitudes, and attributes on your newly devised list of hiring criteria. Try to envision the applicants who might apply to this advertisement. They should be very much like your highest-performing employees.

With the new criteria in mind, there are many selection techniques that can be used.

Pre-Employment Testing

Each additional tool that is used to aid in the selection process improves the chances of selecting the best employee for your organization. There is an abundance of standardized pre-employment tests that can help the selection process along. Some of these are specific to customer service, while others are more diverse and/or job specific. Some pre-employment tests assist by providing customized behavioral-based interview questions.

When we first began to implement a well-organized pre-employment testing process that looked closely at behaviors, we found that turnover in the first year was greatly reduced and the success rate during probationary periods was much, much higher. As you may suspect, the performance issues that can sometimes haunt our daily work began to decrease as well. We found that the time previously spent addressing these issues could now be spent on goals and action plans to move the organization to a better place.

We recommend that organizations, with the assistance of their Employee Experience Teams (see Solution Six), sift through their pre-employment testing to tailor the perfect method to assist in the screening of applicant pools. When doing this, make sure that the test is malleable—able to be shaped to fit not only the skills and technical knowledge of your applicants, but also the newly devised "rock star" criteria of behaviors, attitudes, and attributes.

Bottom line? Seek out a pre-employment testing tool that can screen for the following:

- Behaviors, attitudes, and attributes (personality testing). This screen will allow you a glimpse at what the employee "will do."

- Skills and technical knowledge (ability testing). This screen will allow you a glimpse at what the employee "can do."

Reference Checking

We know this to be true in healthcare (and maybe it is true in other industries as well): organizations tend to pass around the difficult employees to departments within the organization or to other organizations. We need to stop this practice if we are going to achieve peak results!

Healthcare is infamous for investing massive amounts of time dealing with a disruptive physician. After months, sometimes even years, of dealing with a physician who has wreaked havoc on the interior culture on the organization, they part ways, only to find the same physician has quickly engaged in the same exact behaviors in another organization.

Most organizations, including healthcare, require contact with the applicant's references as part of their applicant screening process. Unfortunately, many references provide little to no background information about a candidate. And as we all know, a candidate is also far more likely to list positive references only. Not many are going to give you a list of references that will dash their hopes of being employed.

There are a couple ideas that we advocate in an effort to assuage your reference checking woes:

- Be the change you wish to see in others. Create and adopt a policy, with the help of legal advisors, that empowers your organization to provide thorough, helpful information when asked for references on your current or former employees.

- When you request information on candidates, have the candidate sign a release form that allows you to contact individuals who are sourced outside of just what was listed in the references section of the application. When you dig deeper than just the names listed, you will likely uncover far more helpful reference information.

The timing of conducting reference checking is something to be decided and standardized. Some organizations like to do them before the interview, while others do them just before the employment offer. Jane and I lean toward having reference checks completed before the interview. This allows for the information obtained to be used to formulate precise, personalized interview questions. Checking references beforehand may also turn up a piece of information that makes the interview a null point, saving both time and resources.

Past behavior predicts future behavior.

In this, the modern digital age, the value of social media cannot be overlooked in the selection process. If you choose to gather information in this manner, it is best to develop policies to guide you along the way. As a leader, I admit to having scanned many possible candidates' Facebook pages, sometimes finding a trend of negativity toward coworkers and employers.

Peer Interviews

Truly invested, empowered employees can be a sight to behold. One way in which we help create these vested employees is peer interviewing. When employees help to choose their peers, there is a certain sense of responsibility that comes with the action. These employees model excellent behavior for their hires, train them, and most importantly, share a desire for them to be successful.

I've witnessed two very contrasting scenarios, one without peer interviewing and one with, that helped to cement the positive nature of the practice in my mind. Prior to implementing peer-interview panels, I overheard several housekeepers chatting over lunch. As they conversed about the new employee that was recently hired by their supervisor, negativity abounded.

"Can you believe that she hired him? He can't even show up for work during his orientation! I would never have hired him. We are wasting our time training him!"

Fast-forward to a couple of years later. After implementing peer-interview panels in which housekeeping employees select their new team members, a new scene emerged. Two housekeepers were standing at the time clock. They were clocking out from work that day, fresh in the knowledge of the choice they had made during a recent peer-interview process (both were on the panel). A new employee had just been fired earlier that day during his probationary period. A thoughtful conversation abounds. "Can you believe he fooled us during the interview process? We thought that he would be more dependable. How did we go wrong? What should we do next time?"

Of the two scenarios, there is an obvious positive and negative. The choice to implement peer interviewing is an easy one in my mind.

The choice for who you would want on a peer-interviewing panel is easy as well, and I would bet that there are many names on the list of rock stars you made earlier that would fit the bill. Engage these rock stars, and train them to be excellent peer-interview panel members.

Peer-Interview Panel Tips

1. Have applicants sign the organization's Behavior Standards (more on these standards in Solution

Eight) before they get interviewed. If they balk at the idea, do not advance them to a peer interview.

2. Conduct pre-employment testing prior to the peer interview. You may also want your candidates to answer some customized pre-interview questions. If so, this can be made part of the application process. The more you know about a candidate prior to the interview, the more prepared your interview panel will be.

3. The organization's human resources department and the hiring leader pre-screen applicants prior to the peer panel interview. They will organize applicant information including the application, pre-interview screening, and reference checking. The hiring leader will conduct a screening interview involving behavioral-based interviewing techniques and may also assist in the reference checking. The peer-interview panel receives candidates for interviews only after they have been approved by the hiring leader.

4. A peer-interview panel, populated by your rock stars, should be trained to interview and select their new teammates.

5. The peer-interview process uses behavioral-based interviewing techniques and a selection tool to

facilitate the final decision. We will go over these techniques next in this solution.

6. The peer-interview process may also include a tour of the department and maybe even of the entire organization. These tours, while fun, also ensure that when the candidate is hired, their first day on the job won't be their first day in the workplace. These tours also serve to loosen up the candidate, allowing for deeper insight. How interested do they seem in the organization? How do they interact with employees or customers they meet? Do they ask questions about what they are observing?

Selecting the right candidate to join your team is an important decision, laden with consequences, good or bad. A process for peer interviewing, which includes behavior-based interviewing techniques, will provide great assistance.

Behavioral-based Interviewing

How a person has reacted in the past can be a firm indicator of how they will react in the future. Behavioral-based interviewing questions can examine these indicators.

When determining what you are looking for in an employee, make sure to take the needs of your team, the job, and the characteristics critical to success in the position under consideration. We emphasize here, again, that those behaviors, attitudes, and attributes that are now a major component of your hiring criteria are cornerstones of your behavioral-based questions.

Additionally, we need to move away from the old mind set that, when interviewing three candidates, the same questions need to be posed to all three. If we have done our due diligence in the pre-interview process, we can tailor each interview to the specific candidate. That said, there will be questions that focus on the larger picture and need to be asked of all, but do not shy away from probing with questions that delve deeper into the specific candidate's background.

Sample Behavioral-based Interviewing Questions

1. When working with patients or family members, tell us how you create an environment that helps them feel informed and cared for. Provide a specific example of when you have done this.

2. Tell us about a specific situation when you did not have the knowledge or skill to complete a task or assignment. What did you do? What was the outcome?

3. Describe a time when you exceeded a patient's expectations. What did you specifically do to achieve that outcome?

4. Describe how you contributed to the success of a team of which you were a member.

5. Describe a tough problem at work that involved conflict between individuals or departments. What was your role in the situation? What was the outcome?

Having been part of many peer-interview panels that utilized behavioral-based interviewing techniques, this format can be a big change for the panel members and the candidates. Often candidates want to respond to the question in a manner of, "This is what I would do in this situation," but the real response the panel desires is, "This is what I actually did in the past when faced with this situation." This often requires the skill of redirecting the candidate and probing deeper into his or her response to each question.

To guide this, we recommend that behavioral-based interview questions be responded to with the following information (E.A.R.):

- **Event:** describe the situation that occurred.

- **Action:** describe what actions were taken.

- **Result:** explain the results of the actions.

Employees participating in interview panels should be trained in regard to interviewing and decision-making practices, including the skill of asking probing follow-up questions when a thorough answer is not provided.

Probing Questions for Behavioral Interviewing	
Event	When did the situation start? Over what period of time did this take place? What happened next? Who else was involved?
Actions	What thoughts were going through your mind at the time? What did you do next? What were your reactions when that happened? What did you do? What did you say?
Results	How did the situation turn out? What was the end result? What happened in the short term? What happened in the long term?

Once the peer-interview process is complete, the panel needs to work together to make a hiring decision. These team members may need tools to assist them in discussing and deciding the final outcome of the selection process.

Tools such as the weight-based decision matrix (shown in Appendix 4) can assist in organizing the interview panel's discussions. It is important to remember that when using a decision matrix, the highest score doesn't always mean an instant hire. In fact, the panel should be empowered to come to the conclusion on who is the best fit. In some situations, this may also mean that none of the candidates is the right fit, so the end decision is to continue the search for that new team member.

Hiring in Times of Crisis (Jane's Story)

I faced a time in my career as a leader of two critical care nursing units when I had fourteen of my sixty employees leave me. Most of them were employees who manned the night shift.

I was fortunate enough to have led in a college town with a very high-quality nursing school so that I likely could have replaced all of those nurses quickly enough, but how do you replace the experience and competency of those who left?

I was in a pretty bad way when this span of time hit. I knew I would have to work shifts myself in order for safe patient care to happen. I knew I was also going to have to train new emergency room nurses, most of them fresh out of school.

I worked in an organization with an amazing human resources department. Some leaders I interact with across the country see human resources as a barrier to making quick and effective leadership decisions, but ours was not that way.

I knew they were compliant with the hiring policies for a reason. The reason was so that cowboys like me did not, under hiring pressure, hire the wrong candidates.

Julie was our assistant director in our human resources department. She knew I was going to be on a hiring frenzy and right away pulled up her bootstraps to help me.

Around this time, I was contacted by a nurse named Jim. Jim called me on the phone and stated that he had just moved to the area and was seeking employment. I asked him if he had filled out an application and he replied, "When you hear my credentials you will know why I called you first."

There was the first red flag. In other words, "Let's just cut through the crap. You are going to want me, no matter what."

So, I listened to the fact that he had all the right credentials (e.g., ACLS, TNCC, PALS, SANE), and that he had been a charge nurse in his previous position in a Level 1 trauma center several states away.

As I fought to find napkins in my desk drawer to contain the puddle of drool that was rapidly spreading over my clothing and desktop, I asked if he could come in for a peer interview.

He informed me he had interviews at two neighboring hospitals but could come over "right away" for an interview with me.

Up shot the second red flag. We did peer interviewing in our organization for a reason. Great minds together achieve more than one frontline leader looking down the barrel at several months on the night shift.

So, Jim came in for an interview with me that afternoon. All of his potential peers were working in a very busy emergency room that afternoon and could not break free. I interviewed him myself. Jim's demeanor of "you want me" continued through the interview process.

He was dressed very casually and did not have a resume prepared. Since he had not filled out an application, I had no prior job experiences to look at while he was answering my quickly prepared questions. I did not use behavioral-based interviewing questions. I do not have an excuse for this other than he was right—I did want him to work in my department. That day, preferably!

I let Jim know that he did, indeed, need to fill out an application so that I could begin the hiring process. He reluctantly accompanied me to the human resources office, where I could introduce him to the gang and get an application to fill out. It was on our walk there that Jim casually mentioned that he was only really willing to work night shifts and weekends. Again, drool was pooling at the base of my throat.

This, however, was the third red flag, ignored completely by me. I have worked with some amazing people who just plain like to be present in the hospital when others do not and prefer to work every weekend night shift because that is how they get to work their shifts all in a row, or because they have family commitments during the week. However, those employees can usually voice that to you. Jim offered no explanation other than this is his preferred schedule, end of story. I, of course, told him that would work just fine, as no one else was vying for those shifts.

We parted ways that day with him promising to fill out the application and return it to the human resources department, and me promising him I would call as soon as his references and licensure were verified, usually within one week.

I went about my merry way that day thinking I had a big bonus in my hip pocket, an experienced and competent nurse who would share the pain of splitting the night shifts and weekends with me for the next few months or so. I wondered to myself how he would feel about being a preceptor to train new nurses as soon as he hit the door.

So far had I strayed from what I knew to be an effective leadership practice in hiring that I could not feel impending doom like an elephant on my chest!

My office phone rang a few days later, and it was Julie, the human resources rock star, on the line. She was calling to inform me that I could not hire Jim. I, at that very moment, had Jim on a brief orientation schedule and assigned to training other new employees for the entire summer.

I may have screeched: "WHAT? WHY? Why can't I hire him?"

Julie replied, "None of his past employers will give me a reference. Not even a date of hire, length of service, or acknowledge that he even existed within their organization."

Well, another red flag. Like a bull in the streets of Madrid, I plowed through that one as well.

"Julie, the guy is perfect. There is nothing he cannot do in our emergency room. I need him. There must be a mistake. You must be calling the wrong hospitals or something. You need to start over. I am dying here."

To give credit to Julie, she did not slam the phone in my ear or tell me to take my thumb out of my mouth and quit whining. She stated she would call the hospitals back again and ask to speak to the emergency room directors, or human resources directors, instead of those she spoke to earlier. What she got when she made those phone calls were answers from emergency room directors stating, "You need to call human resources. We cannot talk about employees," and human resources leaders who stated, "Yes, he did work here, and no, we will not provide a reference."

Despite the red flags and lack of a positive reference check, I played upon every ounce of sympathy from those who work above Julie to allow me to hire Jim. I called in every favor I have ever gained as a high-performing leader to get my vice president, Sue, to trust me that we needed to break all the rules on this one hire.

Red flags are there for a purpose. As it turned out, I fired Jim within his ninety-day probationary period for many reasons. Here are a few:

- His preceptor gave up on his orientation within a week. This very savvy emergency room nurse said, "He told me he did not need me and to get out of his way."

- I noted on his documentation that he was taking three to four tries to start an IV and was using the very smallest size catheter every time. If you know anything at all about emergency room nurses, their motto is "go big or go home," and they rarely miss an IV start.

- I showed up in the middle of the night once, as I was known to do, and Jim was not there. I asked his peers where he was and they stated, "He takes off for a period of time every night. We think he goes outside to take a nap in his car. He takes all of his breaks at

once and is gone for an hour." NOT IN MY
EMERGENCY ROOM!

I was waiting for Jim when he reappeared that night, and he
informed me that my emergency room was ridiculously
understaffed, our equipment was crap, and he had never
worked with worse physicians in his career. If he could
not hit the broadside of a barn with an IV start, it was
because my hospital purchased the wrong kind of angio-
caths. It was not his fault. He was considered an expert at
all the other hospitals where he had worked.

Now the white flag waved in my head, and I
dragged myself into Sue's office the next day and asked
her, as my vice president, to assist me in terminating Jim.
Very quickly.

The safety of patients and the quality of care
they received was my primary concern. Second, I
thought of the damage I had done to my relationships
with employees and physicians. They counted on me
to choose wisely when hiring. They counted on me to
involve them in these decisions. What message did I
convey to them by dumping a problem like Jim on them
every weekend?

Regrettably, my relationships with my boss (Sue!)
and Julie from human resources were at risk of being
damaged. I thought of myself first and made the decision that upright and licensed was good enough, forcing
them to see it as good enough as well, even though their
personal judgment was offended.

I damaged my integrity as a leader. You have to
be able to look yourself in the mirror every day in a leadership position, and my mirror was cloudy for a long,
long time.

Building the reputation of being a great organization and a great place to work can reward you with a large applicant pool. This allows you to be selective each time you hire. A well-designed and executed selection process includes pre-interview screening, reference checking, panel interviews, and behavioral-based interviewing techniques. This process is likely the successful candidate's first impression of their new employer. Make it a great one.

The Onboarding Process

The Society for Human Resources Management describes onboarding as the process by which a new hire gets adjusted to the social and performance aspects of their job quickly and smoothly, as well as learns the attitudes, knowledge, skills, and behaviors required to function effectively within the organization.

Best practices for onboarding thoroughly and successfully have been researched to elicit a plethora of benefits, including higher job satisfaction, organizational commitment, and performance level (Ashford and Black, 1996).

Five Key Objectives of Onboarding

1. *Engaging the new employee in the vision and strategies of the organization.* This is the vision for greatness. This is what we do and why we do it. We refer to this as "bringing the mission and vision alive at all levels." This strategic plan is not just for leadership, nor is it a formal document on a shelf.

It needs to be a living idea in everyone's minds, including new employees.

2. *Connecting to the culture of the organization.* This is how we behave, perform, and contribute as members of this organization. These are the standards we uphold in order to achieve peak performance.

3. *Facilitating the establishment of interpersonal relationships and information networks.* Being the new fish in a large pond can be arduous. Don't leave new employees out in the cold. New employees need to be connected to the information and communication networks. New employees need to engage in relationship building.

4. *Increasing clarity, competence, and confidence.* Employees are hired because there is work to be done. Set them up for success with a comprehensive and personalized orientation to promote their mastery in the work they have been hired to do. When it comes to orientation, it isn't always about the quantity—it is about the quality. One size doesn't fit all. It is a balance between standardization and individualization.

5. *Teaching the necessary regulatory, legal, accreditation, and policy requirements.* Each

industry has its own set of such requirements. Some of these requirements are so vital that a new employee must know about them on, or before, their first day at work.

There are many cleverly devised practices for meeting these five objectives. We have found the following ones to be successful:

Make Day One a Special Day

My cousin recently accomplished a lifelong dream. Raising seven children, she has spent years being a dutiful and caring parent. After all this time and wonderful experience, she decided it was time to pursue her dream career in nursing. She completed nursing school, passed the nursing boards with flying colors, and eagerly made her first steps into the world of healthcare.

When I asked her about her first day on the job, I found myself a bit perplexed by her experience. She dove right into explaining how she had attempted IVs and found success after a few missed opportunities. She talked about the mysterious complexity of the electronic health record system. She also spoke about how the employees on this unit had *no idea that she was coming*.

They had no idea.

This was a monumental day for my cousin. A day when she was able to fulfill a childhood dream, to become one of those she had thought heroes. Yet, there she was, expecting to feel special but feeling left alone in the cold.

I've heard far too many stories of those reporting to work on day one, only to find nothing prepared at all. No desk, no chair, no identification badge, no signifier at all that anyone was paying attention to their existence.

This abandonment and alienation can seed itself in the mind of a new employee. To avoid this, we challenge leaders and their employees to find ways to delight new employees on their first day.

One of our partner healthcare organizations, with ever-increasing employee engagement, came up with the following to make every day one special:

- At least one member of their Employee Experience Team personally greets new employees when they arrive for their first day. They present them with a welcome card that has been signed by the team.

- They present the new employees with a welcome candy bar wrapped in customized paper that reads: "Serving size: One Happy Employee" and the ingredients are the organization's standards of excellence.

- They send a welcome package to the homes of the employees addressed to the entire family. This package invites them to be a part of the hospital family and lists events in which they are able to do so.

As this example shows, making the first-day experience special can be placed in the hands of existing employees. This doesn't have to be one more thing on a leader's to-do list. Engage and empower employees to lend a hand in this way.

The First Days' Checklist

Quite often, there are very important elements of orientation that must be completed very soon in the tenure of a new employee. Usually, these are safety-related elements and are often incorporated to meet regulatory and/or legal requirements, thus fulfilling the fifth key objective to successful onboarding.

These elements, due to their critical importance, often are required learning within the first days of employment. You can't leave this to chance. A systematic process that is consistently applied is a must. One tactic to make this happen is to devise a First Days' Checklist and a process for the systematic use of the checklist. A sample of a First Days' Checklist is provided in Appendix 5.

In an organization that recently implemented such a checklist, the leaders who hired employees often found it to be a very helpful tool. Yet, it was the leaders who hired employees very infrequently who were most excited by the First Days' Checklist. When you must do something that is so important, yet something you do infrequently, a checklist such as this is helpful.

Department-specific Orientation

As a vice president of a hospital in which I was administratively responsible for the nursing care delivered in each nursing unit, my team and I attempted to constantly engage our employees and leaders. We encouraged them to investigate, adopt, and continually refine the best nursing care models, policies, and practices to deliver the very best care to our patients. At one point, we made a drastic change in our model of care. It was a multi-year improvement effort that came to include hours upon hours of employee involvement and training.

Along the road toward this change, many new employees joined us to work in these meticulously designed and changing systems. These new employees needed training not just on how we were now doing things, but also on why we deliver care in this manner. To both entice and hammer home the model we were using, we designed department-specific orientation with as much precision and care as we did the original implementation training.

Though it may seem obvious that each position should have a carefully designed orientation path, we happen upon many examples in which this is not the case. This can be accomplished in many different ways:

- *A classroom-style department orientation.* The nursing unit referenced above designed a class that they labeled "Med-Surg 101" in which new employees are grouped together to cover topics like the Patient Care Model, electronic health records, and equipment training.

- *Competency stations.* Hands-on demonstration of competency is desired for certain job skills. If the department already utilizes annual competency skill stations for existing employees, these same stations can be required for new employees soon after their start date.

- *Simulation.* Some organizations are fortunate enough to have access to a simulation center. Not all industries or jobs can benefit from simulation, but in healthcare there is great benefit. If this happens to apply and there is availability of such, simulation should certainly be brought into the orientation fold.

- *Preceptor training courses.* A preceptor is often assigned to assist by training employees during the orientation process. Some organizations require that any employee who is going to serve as a preceptor must attend a preceptor training course. These courses include content on adult learning principles, as well as the organization's policies and procedures for new-hire orientation, onboarding, and the probationary period. Investing in the development of preceptors will benefit them as well as the new employees they train.

Organization-wide Orientation

I recently ran across a statistic that reported that 93 percent of organizations conduct an organization-wide orientation that is either in-person, online, or a combination of the two (Anderson, Cunningham-Snell, and Haigh, 1996).

Jane and I are very familiar with the common practice of hospitals conducting a full-day orientation event at certain intervals, depending on the volume of new employees entering the organization. Many of these organizations require that this be the first day of the new employee's official employment. In this light, they batch together all new employees at the next scheduled orientation event.

We have some concerns when it comes to this orientation

formula. We don't like how it can delay the start of much-needed employees. We like to see the "time to fill" vacant positions kept short. As you are likely to know from the LEAN concepts surrounding waste, batching creates a form of delay; and in this example, a delay in the start date of a much-needed new employee (Lean Institute, 2014).

There is an abundance of other techniques, such as the First Days' Checklist or a component of online orientation, that may help your organization avoid delays in the employee starting process, all while getting the required information to employees early in their orientation. The formal classroom-style organization-wide orientation can still occur on scheduled intervals while at the same time not delaying the start date of new employees.

While the timing of organization-wide orientation events is important, what is included in this orientation is another key consideration. We highly recommend that the majority of this content be focused on meeting the first three key objectives of onboarding:

1. Engaging the new employee in the vision and strategies of the organization.

2. Connecting to the culture of the organization (i.e., this is how we behave, perform, and contribute as members of this organization. These are the standards we uphold to achieve peak performance).

3. Facilitating the establishment of interpersonal relationships and information networks.

In our evaluation of an organization's new hire orientation programs, we often find that the main focus is on onboarding objective 5, which includes regulatory, legal, accreditation, and policy requirements. This often happens at the expense of the onboarding objectives 1, 2, and 3, which are intended to engage new employees in the mission and vision, connect them to the culture, and initiate relationships and information networks.

New Employee Check-Ins

With onboarding objective 3, we want to facilitate the establishment of interpersonal relationships and information networks. Employee rounding, as described in Solution One, is a core leadership tactic that builds relationships. We can gain the benefits of rounding with new employees in the form of a New Employee Check-In discussion.

Sample Questions for New Employee Check-Ins

At thirty days:

- What do you like most about your job? About the organization?

- Are the position and organization meeting your expectations? Provide details.

- Who has been helpful in the orientation period? How have they been helpful?

- On a scale of one to ten, how happy are you working for this organization? If not a ten, what would have to happen to make it a ten?

- Currently, is there anything that would cause you to leave the organization?

- What type of feedback would you like to receive about your performance that you are not receiving now?

- Is there anything else that may be important to you that was not covered in this meeting?

- As your leader, how can I help you?

At ninety days:

- How does the job compare to what you thought it would be?

- Is there any reason why you may feel this is not the right place for you?

- Do you know of anyone who would be a good fit for our organization?

- Is there anything that your previous employer did that you think may work really well here?

- On a scale of one to ten, how happy are you working here? If not a ten, what would need to happen to make it a ten?

- Is there anything else that may be important to you that was not covered in this meeting?

- As your leader, how can I help you?

As the leader of a new employee, there is much that can be harvested from check-in sessions, including recognition opportunities for other employees. This is a great tactic for combating the "eating our young" behaviors that can sometimes surface. During a check-in, you have an opportunity to hear about the warm, welcoming, and helpful employees. In turn, you can recognize and celebrate these helpful employees. This recognition helps to promote the positive behaviors that you want to consistently see toward new employees. What gets recognized and celebrated gets repeated.

Getting-to-Know-You Activities

When leaders round purposefully with employees, they build relationships. We always recommend that leaders round with heart, always trying to leave each rounding session having learned something new about their employee.

A leader forming a relationship with each new employee

is certainly important. Certainly the establishing of interpersonal relationships applies to coworkers as well. What can be done to encourage our employees to get to know each other?

In our travels, we have seen leaders, departments, and members of Employee Experience Teams get especially creative and have fun while devising and engaging in relationship-building activities.

Here are a few ideas to get you started.

1. ***"Getting to Know You" Bulletin Boards.*** While speaking at a national conference, Jane and I were talking with a leader about an excellent idea her team had recently applied. Her team had dedicated a bulletin board, in a prominent place in their department, designated as the "Getting to Know You" board. This was a place for employees to share information about themselves. This sharing was organized around changing themes. Some great ideas for themes are: Where in the world are you from? What was your first job? What hobby are you passionate about? She also shared with us that, to keep it fresh and lively, they changed the theme of the board every few weeks, the color scheme would update as the theme updated, and the team would often arrange to have a new theme put up after-hours so as to surprise the employees when they arrived for work.

2. ***Mystery Employee Game.*** One of our partner organizations uses their quarterly leadership training sessions to learn more about their leaders. Each leaders submits a

little known fact and himself/herself to the organizer. These facts are displayed throughout the day and leaders use an answer sheet to guess which mystery snippet belongs to each respective leader. In keeping with the levity of the game, a silly prize is given to whoever answers the most correctly. This game can be easily played among employees. I read that the successful company Zappos uses the sign-on prompt for their information system to engage employees in a coworker guessing game. Given a little thought, there are many ways this mystery game could be played out.

3. *New Employee Fact Sheets.* A simple question and answer sheet that is meant to learn more about new employees (e.g., favorite color/treat/beverage, nickname, how they like to be recognized and communicated with, etc.) is another easy-to-use tactic. This information, along with a photo, can be displayed on a new-employee board. This helps both coworkers and leaders to surprise new employees with something that will make them feel welcome. I found this information useful well beyond the orientation period. For instance, when I would have a scheduled meeting with one of my employees, I could surprise them by having their favorite beverage and treat awaiting them.

You might be thinking, "I can't add one more thing to my to-do list." Time to delegate, engage, and empower! There will be employees on your team who will be eager to organize the "Getting-to-Know-You Activities." I've always found this to be true.

Probationary Period Evaluation

A formal orientation evaluation often signals the end, or an extension, of orientation. We encourage leaders to pay special attention to the orientation period, using it to determine if someone is a good fit for the position (behavior, attitude, skill, etc.). New employees should take this time to do the same.

A common length of an orientation or probationary period is ninety days. This can be longer when the position taken is highly specialized. This period is crucial assessment time. Even if we apply some of the best hiring techniques that we know, we can still make the wrong choice. The probationary period is when we figure this out.

If you find that your new employee just isn't working out, we advise that you do not extend the probationary period unless there is a very high chance that the orientation objectives will be met with a small extension of time. We have seen this needed extension be warranted in highly technical roles.

If the problem areas identified during the probationary period fall under behavior and attitude, we highly recommend ending employment prior to the completion of the probationary period. Skill change can be easy. Behavioral change rarely is.

Leaders must be mindful of compliance with the specific time frames in their organizations involving probationary periods. I spent two decades of my time in leadership in a unionized hospital environment. The negotiated agreements between the hospital and the union clearly articulated the end of a probationary period. Far too often, I experienced situations in which leaders had not paid proper attention to the time frame for extending the orientation or making the choice to let the new hire go. In some instances, since no decision was made within the proper time frame, the employee was seen as having successfully completed the probationary period. Whether or not that was the truth is irrelevant. By default, it was a matter of time, not evaluation. Leaders must have a system for keeping track of these important dates and heed them.

Once you've selected and hired a new employee, the decision-making process continues into the probationary period. Use the probationary period wisely to orient your employees well to set them up for success. If it doesn't work out, utilize your probationary period and rights correctly.

Celebrating Successful New Employees

Organizations should develop a way to positively recognize when new employees have finished their orientation period. It is best practice to recognize their preceptors as well, either at the same time or at a designated recognition event.

Here are some recognition ideas for new employees who have succeeded at meeting the orientation objectives:

- Orientation completion certificate—hand-delivered by the CEO

- Employee badge changing ceremony (if probationary badge was used)

- Gift of company logo-wear

▪ Breakfast with the CEO

▪ Recognition in company newsletter or on a designated bulletin board

A Case Study of Onboarding

In the work that we do with healthcare organizations across the country, Jane and I have come face-to-face with the struggle to obtain peak performance. In one of our recent journeys, we came across an organization in which an annual employee engagement survey, of which nearly 90 percent of employees had participated, pointed to opportunities for improvement of the onboarding process. While certain indexes of employee engagement and satisfaction were going up, this one was heading down.

These results were puzzling to all of us. Many of the processes that were integrated into the onboarding process were considered to be industry best practices. When these leaders reached out to us, they were intent on completely revamping their onboarding process to turn the results around.

Jane and I dug further into the issue and the employee engagement survey data. We dug down from the organization level to the departmental level. We discovered that this was where the problem, and the answer, could be found. We found that in most departments of the hospital, the employee satisfaction with the onboarding process was rated at 100 percent, signifying that new employees were very satisfied. Yet, there were a few departments in which the onboarding process was rated extremely low. These new employees from a few departments had generated enough low responses to skew the entire result toward the negative.

With this discovery it was easier to assess:

1. What were the 100 percent satisfied departments doing well with their onboarding process?

2. What were the onboarding practices of the low-performing departments?

Needless to say, a complete overhaul of the organization's onboarding practices did not make it to the action plan. It simply wasn't needed. The plan to improve was instead focused on pairing successful departments with those that needed help. In essence, the organization as a whole had great processes for onboarding. They just weren't adopted by all departments.

When we work with organizations to adopt best practices, we often see pockets of success and pockets of opportunity. Until the organization reinforces the policy of "this is how we do it around here" (e.g., the best practices are adopted by all), there will continue to be mixed results.

Keeping Track

Research published in 2014 showed that 24 percent of employees leave within the first year. Additional research shows that half of all hourly workers will leave a new job in the first four months (Shah, Pollack, and Dutta 2014). Keeping track of certain statistics is helpful to gauge the results of your efforts toward high-quality hiring and onboarding processes.

We recommend that organizations, and individual departments, monitor the following:

- Number of new employees who leave within the first ninety days and within the first year

- Reasons for new employees who leave within the first ninety days and within the first year

- Number of new employees who have extended probationary periods

- Reasons for extension of probationary periods

- Employee satisfaction or engagement by years of service

- Employee satisfaction or engagement with the onboarding process

- Time it takes to fill open positions

- Vacancy rate

For the monitors that you select, it is helpful to monitor over time and compare to your goal or target. Comparing and benchmarking your results with other organizations or national norms can prove helpful too. These monitors provide feedback on how your selection and onboarding processes are working and what opportunities may exist to make them better.

Call to Action

Given the expense of the hiring process, the cost of a bad hire, and the expense and disruption of turnover, hiring right and onboarding successfully are a must. The expectation is that if you "hire tough" you can "manage easy."

Take the time to assess your current hiring and onboarding practices. See if there are opportunities to take these processes to greater levels and produce excellent results for your organization. The following Hiring and Onboarding Success Plan can serve as a guide through this discovery process:

Hiring and Onboarding Success Pan

Evaluate Current State

- Round with your newest employees. Ask them about their application, interviewing, and onboarding experience.

- Evaluate trends in recent years related to employee satisfaction or engagement data and comments for employees in their first year of employment.

- Evaluate baseline data: Turnover of employees in first ninety days; Turnover of employees in first year; Number of probationary period extensions (successful/ unsuccessful); Time to fill positions; Vacancy Rate

- Review current job descriptions for clarity of expectations of behavior, performance of job tasks, and contributions as well as qualifications.

- Seek understanding of the current pre-hiring processes (e.g., pre-employment testing, reference checking, hiring criteria and job qualifications, interview process and questions, background checks, etc.).

- Seek understanding of current onboarding processes (e.g., department-specific orientation, organization-wide orientation, day one and getting-to-know-you activities, preceptor training and assignment, welcoming activities, probationary period, new employee evaluation process, etc.).

Plan and Make Improvements— Select and Prioritize Based on Assessment

- Create a systematic practice to purposefully round with your newest employees. Conduct Thirty- and Ninety-Day New Employee Check-Ins. Round with purpose and heart and follow up on what you learn.

- Ongoing—Evaluate trends in recent years related to employee satisfaction or engagement data and comments for employees in their first year of employment. Monitor data compared to baseline data: Turnover of employees in first ninety days; Turnover of employees in first year; Number of probationary period extensions (successful/unsuccessful); Time to fill positions; Vacancy Rate.

- Complete Probationary Evaluations on time. Give careful consideration of any probationary extensions.

Never extend probationary periods when the deficiency is in the area of attitude or behavior. Develop a system for keeping track of these important timelines.

- Revise job descriptions to clearly define expectations of behavior, performance of job tasks, and contributions.

- Determine the criterion that exemplifies your top performers. Use this as your criterion when devising behavioral-based interview questions for peer panel interviews.

- Assemble and train a peer interview team. Revise the interview process to include screening by leaders and the human resources department prior to any peer panel interviews.

- Improve onboarding processes (e.g., department-specific orientation, preceptor training and assignment, welcoming activities, etc.).

Evaluate and Adjust

- Regularly review the information from rounding (subjective) and data (objective) to evaluate if the changes are leading to improvements. Adjust plan and improvement activities as necessary. Solution Twelve can guide in these activities.

Leading a Multigenerational Workforce

People resemble their times
more than they resemble
their parents.
—Arab Proverb

Never before in the history of modern workforce has there been such a diverse set of generations working side by side. Your awareness and knowledge of the generational differences in your workplace is another leadership tool in your toolbox. Your use of the tool can assist you in truly understanding what is going to motivate your employees to work at a higher level of engagement. Armed with this knowledge, you can lead an engaged workforce that contributes to the day-to-day operations of your department *and* to the development of winning strategies that will lead to peak performance.

Developing relationships with those who work for you, and with you, should be focused on understanding what makes them tick. Understanding how employees may differ from your beliefs about work is very important in developing great relationships. Any tool in your leadership toolbox that promotes engagement through deeper understanding of your employees is a great one to have. The upside is that learning about the generational differences can be fun too.

Keeping in mind that your employees spend a vast amount of their waking hours at work, they deserve a great place to work. We know from experience that an engaged workforce is a happy, loyal workforce. Gallup's research published in the "State of the American Workplace" report shows that disengagement is costing the United States an estimated $450 billion to $550 billion annually. This focus on leading a multigenerational workforce is aimed at assisting leaders to motivate employees to work at a higher level of engagement.

So, how does all this magic happen? You have already read the rounding information in Solution One, and I cannot stress enough how rounding is the primary way to make your employees feel appreciated and heard. Developing relationships and gaining insight into what motivates and engages employees relies heavily on one-on-one conversations. Rounding provides these interactions.

Though rounding is vitally important, Sue and I have found that elevating the strengths of the diverse generations in the workforce can lend itself to the same ideal. Your employees will find learning about each other fun, and they will come to embrace those aspects of the times that they have in common, as well as the differences that make them unique.

I felt compelled to write a solution on leading the generations in our workforce for many reasons. First, past trainings that I have facilitated with leaders and employees on this topic have always been received as valuable and useful. I firmly believe that the reason for this is that the multigenerational "elephant in the room" has haunted many a workplace for the past few decades.

Leaders and employees tend to look at each other's differences and point to them as a cause for poor performance, or failure, in the workplace instead of looking to them as a method for gaining success. We should be celebrating the generations! Be thankful for the differences! It makes for a powerful team when we can embrace our differences, collaborate, and focus on what we can each uniquely bring to the table to achieve peak results.

Another reason I feel compelled to encourage a deeper appreciation of the generations is that a key driver of engagement is acknowledging what makes your employees tick; this may differ from what motivates you in the workplace. Understanding the generational differences is just one more way to view others for the individuals that they are.

Every one of us has been defined by the environment in which we were raised. However, the events of the world around us mold our very being. The music we hear, the clothes we wear, the culture we were raised in, all of it permeates us, defines us.

Throughout this solution, key points about each generation will be overviewed. Keep in mind that the descriptions of the generations have been researched and are largely the same throughout published literature on this topic. However, how you view yourself, and how your employees view themselves, may be different from the generational "norm." As I have led workshops on this topic, I encountered audience members that feel more closely aligned with a generation different from their own. That is completely okay! Coming to these realizations and understandings is what we are striving for.

The key facets of each generation that we will explore are: (1) a basic understanding of what world forces formed each generation; (2) the general work beliefs of each; and (3) the communication styles inhabited by a generation.

The common threads that hold throughout each generation bind us together in ways yet to be discovered. There is no direct answer to the generational gaps in the workplace, but if we can strive to understand our differences, perhaps we can learn to better accept each other.

The Millennial

Let's start with a look at our newest generation, the millennial generation. A millennial is defined as having been born between 1981 and 2000. The state of our world during these years shaped these minds as follows:

- Technology, technology, technology! Millennials are known as the "clicker" generation.

- Technology has driven this generation further from face-to-face conversation and closer to communication through online means (eg., text, email, IM, Twitter, etc.).

- They were raised in homes in which both of their parents worked, potentially to the detriment of their central family structure. As a result, they insist on work-life balance.

- They are able to network (even globally) without actually having to speak with anyone.

- They work with energy and enthusiasm, likely because they focus on work-life balance.

- Events like 9/11 and Columbine have shaped their worldview. Schools, offices, and places outside of the home are not perceived as "safe" places.

In the workplace, employees from the millennial generation do not feel that there needs to be a set time for them to work prior to being promoted to a leadership role. Given that one of the key drivers of employee engagement is providing a clear career path for your employees, your millennial employees likely need a defined career path more than any other generation. Also, their view on "the team" being the primary driver of workplace achievement, rather than "the boss," really positions them for success in twenty-first-century leadership.

If your workplace hasn't adopted a formal career planning, succession planning, or mentoring process, then engage in informal leadership development such as delegation and progressive work assignments. Utilize time during rounding to engage in discussion regarding career goals and development or educational desires.

Let's overview more of what has been discovered about millennials in the workplace:

- They do not view the workplace as a hierarchy. The workplace to them is a team that collaborates on any given day, on any given task in front of them.

- They tend to use their personal passions as fuel to work on independent projects.

- They pride themselves on their ability to multitask. This stems from having multiple conversations at once via their chosen technology. Often, they are reaching out to others while they are at work.

- Direct, interpersonal conversations may be difficult.

- They will often look to others who have gone before them and who may have the same issues as a mentor.

- They prefer communication via technology. A phone call or a request for direct conversation may not be answered, but a text will be.

How can you effectively lead a millennial considering these common traits? The most obvious answer is to make sure to engage them anytime you are looking to do anything with technology. They understand it and can bridge the knowledge of the newest technology available with how it will work for you.

Celebrate the energy and passion for what they do outside of work by having them apply it in the workplace. You learn of their interests when forming a relationship with them through rounding.

And, if you ever are challenged with celebrating your

employee group, let your millennial employees serve as your chief party officers. Whenever a goal is attained or an achievement accomplished, give them a budget and let them loose!

Additionally, when decision-making with millennials, ask for a consensus. Recall that millennials rarely observe hierarchy in the workplace. They want to be valued for their ideas. This may take more time for decision-making but truly is the way to engage this employee group to their fullest.

Communication Tips: Millennial

- TEXT! Short, direct communication is always a good bet. In fact, if you are like me and have given birth to a cadre of millennials, you had better learn to text in order to communicate with your children.

- Emailing is the second preferred method of communication. Millennials tend to have their phones near, but they rarely answer them. Cell phones to them are a mode of quick, efficient communication but not through speech.

- You will find that your rounding sessions with a millennial tend to go a bit differently. They are very results-oriented. They love to work for an organization or department that "keeps track." Expect them to ask you questions about how their team is meeting their goals.

A great example of engaging millennials in the workplace is when Sue, as our hospital's chief nursing officer, led a multidepartmental team of nurses to work on implementing a new process of Bedside Shift Reporting. This was a vital team for improving safety, yet challenging because it was essentially throwing out the way nurses had been communicating with each other (and their patients) for years! Needless to say, it was quite the hot topic. It was viewed with negativity and suspicion by many.

Wisely, Sue led the creation of a diverse team, representing multiple generations, nursing units, and shifts. As the work of the team ensued, Sue identified that there were three millennials on the team who were extremely passionate about making this change happen in their work environment. While she included all of the team members in the decision-making for this new practice, Sue delegated the training of all nurses to these three engaged millennials. Sponsoring them with her stamp of approval, her leadership message was very clear: "This is going to happen, and these are our champions. They are going to teach us, inspire us, and support us through this change." These three young nurses were looked upon with respect, and their enthusiasm about the change was contagious.

A frequent comment I hear from leaders is "I don't understand the millennials." This lack of understanding is likely due to the differences in generations. For generations, people have been differing from each other. The millennials have so much to offer, as do all of the generations. When you consider that millennials are major contributors to important work in your department (and may take your position as a leader when you leave it!), it pays to develop a relationship and communication style that works for them and you.

Generation X

Given the positive attributes of Generation X, it is well worth your time to explore what makes them tick to engage them at new levels. The Gen Xers have long been thought of as the "middle child" in terms of modern generations.

Since Gen Xers tend to make up a small portion of each workforce, it is likely that the predominant feel of your team won't have Gen X attributes. Your team may feel like one big mass of baby boomers and millennials mashed together. Find the Gen Xer in the mix. We all need the strengths of the Gen Xers contributing on our team.

Let's take a look at what world forces have shaped the Gen Xers (born between 1965 and 1980):

- They were affected by corporate downsizing across the country. These events have made them cautious of singular loyalty to an employer.

- They saw burnout and fatigue happen to their parents, so they choose to embody a lifestyle devoid of monetary focus.

- They heard both teachers and parents worry aloud about recession, inflation, and stock market crashes, adding to hesitancy where money is concerned.

- Many experienced divided families and homes during their formative years.

A key strength of Gen Xers in the workplace is their affinity for data. Teams often benefit from those people who love a good problem they can solve by diving into the data. What better person for your quality team than a Gen Xer? Also, a Gen Xer often prefers to work alone or in a very small group. You may find them gravitating toward independent work environments and smaller departments or work groups.

What can you likely expect of Generation X employees in the workplace?

- They are flexible and self-reliant.

- They thrive in the midst of chaos and change.

- They love achieving measurable results, streamlining systems, and improving process efficiency. This makes them your go-to people in data analysis!

- They want to work for an organization that looks at results and achieves them.

- They prefer to work alone or in a very small group.

- They appreciate independent work environments.

- They are extremely tech-savvy and are usually multitasking several projects at once.

- Home and family obligations take up just as much time as work.

Communication Tips: Generation X

- Much like the millennial, texting and email are preferable for this generation. Yet, they engage in personal communication (i.e., face-to-face or phone) on important issues.

- Gen Xers like communicating about data. Rely on them to help communicate results and data to their peers. You may improve your communication with them if you include graphs, tables, and charts.

Generation Xers may likely be a hidden gem within your organization. Search them out amid the clamoring millennials and baby boomers, and engage their strengths. Your team will thank you for it!

Baby Boomers

Most work cultures are dominated by the traits of the generation represented by the greatest numbers. For most modern work cultures, that is the baby boomer generation. That said, this may not last much longer as the boomers are set to retire and the tech-savvy millennials and Gen Xers get set to take the reins.

In the meantime, the boomers make up the vast majority of the modern workforce, and this is not a bad thing by any means. Boomers tend to focus on service and excellence in all they do. They have been raised in an environment of quality and hard work. They feel that leadership is a natural sequence in their career. If they choose to not partake in a leadership position, they still show respect for the title and the responsibility that comes with it.

World events that shaped the baby boomer generation (born between 1946 and 1964) include:

- Vietnam War

- Woodstock

- Kennedy's assassination

- Women's liberation

- Dr. Benjamin Spock introduces "understanding" parenting

A boomer who is considering retirement because they are a certain age or feel they "have to" may be experiencing some separation anxiety. Work gives purpose and meaning to many of us. If you have an employee set to retire who does not have a plan for their retirement, he or she may indeed be very anxious. Make sure you round with these very valuable employees regularly. They may have some great ideas about their future and how your department can benefit.

Sue and I advocate that employers have a great "slow down" plan for their employees nearing retirement. These employees may rise up to the occasion for shifts no one wants or extra projects that need to be done. All they really wanted was a "plan." The plan may be to continue working but with fewer hours and different responsibilities at work.

With long-tenured employees, you may have a challenge on your hands as some may be presenting signs of burnout. While working in many different organizations, I have seen leaders "hang on" to employees who are exhibiting bad behaviors purely out of respect for their time rendered. It is imperative to remember that burnout is a work problem, not a personality problem. You owe it to your boomers to let them know when their behavior is negatively affecting their coworkers.

More about the traits of baby boomers in the workplace:

- Boomers tend to identify with what they do for a living. This is reflected in long work hours and working through personal time.

- Strong team orientation.

- Belief in servant leadership and participative management styles.

- Pride in strong work ethic.

- Emotional maturity.

- Good verbal communication skills.

While the boomer is still working, it is best to pair them with a millennial, either on a team or in a mentoring role. The millennials that are new to their position will need to develop critical thinking skills, and learning from a boomer's work experience can be a huge boon in this regard. This matchup can also serve as a soothing balm for boomer burnout and will also allow the boomer to learn some tech-savviness in an environment that is comfortable for them.

The pairing of a boomer with a millennial works for both when the learning is reciprocated. When I mentored a new employee, I was amazed at how much he had to teach me. I spent a lot of time role modeling great communication with internal and external customers and how to problem solve difficult situations. He spent a lot of time teaching me the shortcuts in the technology we were surrounded with. We both benefited from working together. This sort of intentional pairing may take some planning, preparation, and mentoring from the leader. Mentor your experienced boomers to be accepting of the differences of their millennial partners and vice versa.

Communication Tips: Baby Boomers

- Phone calls

- Personal interaction

Much different from the Gen Xers and millennials, the boomers do appreciate verbal interaction. While they are becoming savvy with email and texting (out of necessity to communicate with their children and grandchildren!), they prefer a face-to-face conversation or a phone call.

One thing that the AARP states about boomers in the workplace is that they value retirement as a means to keep working, just on their own terms. They choose to promote work as a vehicle for their worth, so they may have a difficult time with retirement. A boomer may also choose a new career in retirement completely different from the one they worked in for thirty years. I worked side by side with many a very tenured boomer and have been told, "I think in my next career, I am going to arrange flowers!"

Thank a boomer for continuing to work! Engage their strong team orientation, pride, strong work ethic, emotional maturity, and verbal communication skills to the benefit of the team.

The Traditionalist

Tom Brokaw coined the traditionalist generation, or those born before 1945, as the "Greatest Generation." Through the many trials and tribulations that this generation faced, it is not hard to see why they have been coined as such.

You may have traditionalists in your workforce or department that chose to stay working for fulfillment reasons, the stock market crash, or a loss of retirement funding. Despite the reason, having seasoned veterans as part of the workforce brings a wealth of knowledge and skill, as well as a rich awareness of tradition and history.

So what was happening in the world that shaped the traditionalist generation?

- World War II

- Korean War

- Jackie Robinson joined Major League Baseball

- Disney produced its first animated film

- The Great Depression

- The organization of unions

As a leader, it would behoove you to be aware that tradition-alists may have the notion that you want them "put out to pasture," or that they "make higher wage and can be replaced for less money." Reassurance, as well as showing appreciation for the strengths of the older worker, is always a good practice.

Coaching an employee who may be the same age as your parents can be an especially difficult challenge for a young leader. I worked with a nurse early in my leadership career who loved to point out at the start of every performance appraisal meeting the fact that she could have given birth to me.

Be certain that when there are new pieces of equipment or new technologies being introduced into your workplace there are plenty of educational opportunities for your traditionalists. I was once in an educational session on a new monitoring system with two millennials who were moving ahead of me in the agenda of the class. Even the instructor was struggling to keep up with them! Technology is second nature to millennials, and sometimes they have no idea how quickly their fingers are moving. I was frustrated right up until the point in which I reached out to these two young nurses and asked for their help.

As previously stated about the boomers, you may have a traditionalist that desires a change in their work life but cannot imagine not working. Use rounding as a tool to listen and plan with these employees.

While teaching a leadership training session at a large healthcare organization, we were focused on the quality, service, and safety initiatives the nursing units were struggling to put in place. At one point in the day, a leader spoke up to share a great practice. She explained that she leads the birth center for her hospital. She utilizes a team of retired nurses as volunteers in her department to get many of these key initiatives done. Why not? These are registered nurses with years of experience who can contribute in a place that they love. We applaud these types of solutions.

The traits of the traditionalist in the workplace:

- Very loyal to one employer.

- Believes that retirement means a gold watch after a certain length of time.

- Loyal to country and family first.

- They value hierarchy at work and are respectful of leadership and decisions made by leaders.

Communication Tips: Traditionalists

- Face-to-face interactions

- Written memos

- Thanks in a newsletter or in written communication (thank-you notes!)

- Phone conversations

166

The bottom line with a traditionalist is that you should feel fortunate to have one still working for you. You need to communicate this gratitude often as they are a living legacy to their profession. We stand upon what they have built and are able to continue growing our craft because of what they helped to build.

There is a principle in Servant Leadership that is called "foresight." In order to truly have foresight and be effective at planning, you need to be able to look back and see what worked in your profession or department before. Your traditionalists can help you see these events, if you choose to draw them out in this way.

Generating Results with a Multigenerational Workforce

We want people to be like us and to like us. Thinking that others do not like us can bring tension to the workplace. When there is work to be done and your employees need to collaborate on a decision, recognize that there may be tension at the table when multiple generations are present. It is key to view those you lead as *people,* not shift fillers or mass producers.

The benefits that come from having a multigenerational workforce are plentiful. The diversity represented by employees of multiple generations spawns creativity and a fresh look at problem solving. Having different generations on your team creates flexibility and increases attraction from your customers.

A great way to address a multigenerational work group is to say: "All of us have strengths we bring to the team. Some of us are tech savvy and others know the history of decisions that haven't worked before. All of us are going to create something new and excellent together!"

I am in no way saying that you need to make hiring decisions based on filling the generational gap. This would be a human resources nightmare! However, given that you likely already have employees from multiple generations on your team, you will want to make sure that each generation is represented in your project teams.

Understanding the individuals that represent the diverse generations in your workforce is not just fringe knowledge; it is another effective tool in your leadership toolbox. If getting to know your employees, knowing what makes them tick, and knowing what is going to motivate them to perform at a higher level seems a daunting task, break it down into the manageable activities of rounding and recognition.

- Round daily. Make sure each and every employee has one-on-one time with you monthly (small departments) or quarterly (larger departments). Ask them during rounding how they prefer to be communicated with.

- Voice appreciation for each and every person, no matter their generation. Knowing their generational traits can help you know "what to say" and how best to communicate your appreciation.

I would also encourage you to engage your employees in developing a deeper understanding and appreciation of the generational strengths and differences. One tactic I have found extremely effective is the team-building exercise described below.

Generational Team-Building Exercise

Divide your team into generational groups. Start by providing an overview of the generational traits introduced throughout this solution, leaving out the communication preferences that are listed in the Communication Tips.

Instruct each group to discuss and prepare a group response to the following questions:

- What would you add to the description of your generation?

- How do you like the ideas for change presented to you? What role do you like to have in a change project?

- What is your definition of great communication?

- What is your definition of a great boss?

- What strengths do you feel your generation brings to the team?

Conclude this session by facilitating a discussion surrounding each of the generations and their responses to the questions above. Another great resource that your employees may enjoy reviewing in follow-up to this session is the AARP resource "Leading a Multigenerational Workforce."

Have fun leading your diverse employees! You will start to see that the generational gap becomes a form of bonding between the different generations, not the strict dividing line it once was.

Call to Action

Strengthening awareness and understanding surrounding your diverse workforce can be a powerful leadership tactic as you strive for peak performance. Seek to understand the generational impact and how to leverage this for greatness.

Take the time to assess the current practices surrounding generational diversity. Identify your opportunities to take these practices to higher levels. The following Success Plan can serve as a guide through the discovery process:

Multigenerational Workforce Success Plan

Evaluate Current State

- Seek out any documents that relate to diversity, including generational diversity, in your workplace. Look at handbooks, policies, vision and values statements, etc.

- Seek out understanding of the current education, training, and awareness activities of your organization related to generational diversity.

■ Review applicable employee survey results looking for strengths and opportunities related to generational diversity.

■ Reflect on your personal leadership in the past year. Reflect on the positives that have resulted from a diverse workforce. Reflect on the struggles that are present due to the same. Consider your communication and engagement approaches related to employees of different generations.

■ Review the membership of teams and councils. Does the membership reflect the diversity in the workforce?

Plan and Make Improvements— Select and Prioritize Based on Assessment

■ Commit (or recommit) to employee rounding. Or, refresh your employee rounding with a focused discussion on improving generational understanding and impact.

■ Schedule an employee workshop to promote generational understanding and team building.

■ Create a formal communication plan (or edit your current one) taking into consideration generational communication differences.

- Seek out opportunities daily to provide feedback on behavior, performance, and contributions. Keep in mind the guidance of the three-to-one compliments-to-criticism ratio and generational preferences in regard to feedback.

- Update the membership of teams and councils to mirror the diversity in your workforce. When forming new teams or councils, proactively strive for diversity in membership.

- **Organization Change Agent:** Advocate for an organization-wide diversity plan.

Evaluate and Adjust

- Regularly reassess to evaluate if the changes are leading to improvements. Adjust plan and improvement activities as necessary. See Solution Twelve for additional guidance.

The Employee Experience Team

Bill Taylor, in a *Harvard Business Review* article that referenced the very successful Southwest Airlines, stated that you can't create something special, distinctive, and compelling in the marketplace unless you build something special, distinctive, and compelling in the workplace.

If there is no clear strategy with a dedicated individual or team specifically responsible for creating a special, distinctive, and compelling employee experience, it will likely not happen simply by chance.

We will describe in this solution the creation of a dedicated team, an Employee Experience Team, that can support your organization in a journey to greatness. We recommend that this be an organization-wide team. Yet, some organizations are not ready to go there. If yours isn't, apply this solution within your span of control. Make your work unit the most amazing place to work, and your reputation as such will undoubtedly spread. The hope would be that this would then result in an organization-wide application. You can be an agent of positive change.

Organizing and Leading the Efforts

Organizations we have worked with have found great success in the creation of an Employee Experience Team. This team develops and implements ideas leading to a more engaged and satisfied workforce and increases the organization's ability to recruit and retain talented employees. This team strives to develop an employee experience that encourages desired employees to stay.

From an example outside of healthcare, let's look at LinkedIn. They describe their Employee Experience Team as the team that "Creates inspirational and transformational employee experiences that reinforce LinkedIn's culture and inspires employees to be active participants in creating and nurturing the culture. A.K.A. The best job you will ever have!"

This comes straight out of an advertisement in which they were recruiting for a new team chair. This advertisement went on to list many of the roles and responsibilities of the team, such as these two: "champion new ideas and opportunities to fuel our company culture," and "this is a roll-up-your-sleeves role and you will have the opportunity to develop and own new programs."

This truly speaks to the empowerment of this team to do great things for the employee experience and the organization.

You may think that this is a team of leaders in the

organization. Yet, this is not the case in our experience, nor is it what we recommend. The team may include a leader or two, but it works best when it is employee-populated and employee-driven.

Having a leader as a chairperson is helpful in navigating the organization's processes and can, therefore, assist the team in achieving their purpose. Without some leader involvement, a team of employees can get bogged down in navigating the bureaucracy of the organization when attempting to create change. Also, the team may need access to resources of talent and money. A leader can assist in this way as well.

The leader who sponsors, chairs, or facilitates this team is usually a human resources department leader or employee relations manager. However, any leader with a history of high employee satisfaction and low employee turnover would be a good choice to serve in this role.

In some organizations, they include the role of an Executive Sponsor. This is a senior leader who the team can count on for ongoing support and guidance. The Executive Sponsor may not attend team meetings on a regular basis, yet is committed to keeping up on the activities of the team and assisting when needed by the team.

It is advisable that the Employee Experience Team chairperson makes a multi-year commitment to serve as the chairperson, as this consistency is helpful for team success. However, if a chairperson is not able to recommit, or is not effective in the role, the organization should facilitate replacement of the chairperson. A vice-chairperson could also be selected if the organization chooses and is a good idea for succession planning.

In our partner healthcare organizations, we create several teams in a similar fashion to the Employee Experience Team. The structure is designed to serve as "a hierarchy outside of the normal hierarchy." The purpose of this structure is to aid the organization in achieving its key strategies via teams of engaged employees. In the structure shown below, the chairperson of the Employee Experience Team will serve on the Steering Team to help coordinate the efforts of achieving their goals.

TEAM STRUCTURE

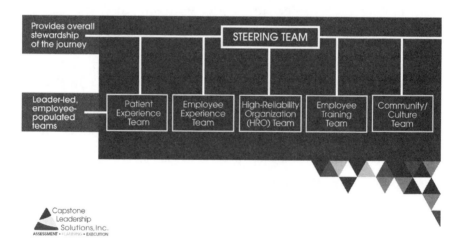

In organizations without this type of team structure, the Employee Experience Team chair may provide regular updates of the team's activities and results to a group of senior leaders. This should be a minimum of quarterly, but preferably monthly updates.

Engaging Employees in the Efforts

The remaining team membership is made up of employees. Not every work unit or department will have an employee on the team, but a cross section should be represented. Don't miss an opportunity to include team members from various shifts and campuses.

Some organizations create a commitment letter in which the team members commit to the responsibilities of the team, including the dedication of their time. We have seen situations in which the employee also receives a signed commitment from their direct supervisor that indicates their support of their employee's involvement on the team. These documents may be added later if there is decreased participation from team members or perceived lack of support from the employee's supervisor.

At the start of each year, the team should ask each member to recommit. If unable to recommit, the member should be replaced by the team. It is helpful to have a level of stability and longevity on the team, as well as a healthy level of new members over time.

When initially forming an Employee Experience Team, query leaders regarding employees that have the qualities of a great Employee Experience Team member. Use these recommendations to select a team of ten to twelve members. In the future, when adding or replacing team members, the team will take on the responsibility of recruiting new members.

In organizations that have had a long history of having a robust and successful Employee Experience Team, it is a coveted team to be recruited to. The team may have many interested and qualified applicants vying for membership, so having a process for new team member selection may be something that the team must develop.

Qualities of Team Members

- Believes in and supports the mission, vision, and strategies of the organization. And supports that changes and improvements are necessary and important to the success of the organization.

- Willing and able to follow through on action assignments.

- Committed to role modeling the behavioral standards that are expected of everyone in the organization.

- High performers (your rock stars) who want to be part of a high-performing team and organization.

- Able to work well in a group setting.

The team, as an early action item, will want to develop a team charter (see example in Appendix 6) that details such things as their purpose and their membership. This team charter, along with annual team goals, are reviewed at the start of each year and as new members join the team.

As part of the initial charter development, a team name

will have to be decided upon. You can see how creative some teams get about their choice of a team name: The Voice, We Matter Here Team, Staff Matter Here Team, and EAGLES (Employee Actions Guiding Long-term Employee Satisfaction). In organizations in which these teams have been highly effective, you can see evidence that the teams are branded positively in the organization. Employees speak of these teams with understanding and respect for the role that they serve, and it becomes highly coveted to be a member.

Team Efforts

Tammy Erickson, who was named as one of the top fifty global business thinkers, states that one of the most powerful approaches to strengthen meaning in the workplace is the creation of "signature experiences." These are highly visible, distinctive elements of the employees' experience that lead to higher levels of engagement and retention.

What are some of these signature experiences that the Employee Experience Team can create? For starters, the team should develop, revise, or revitalize the organization's behavior standards to support the pursuit of excellence. Once standards have been clearly set, articulated, and committed to, the team then keeps them alive by such activities as incorporating them into hiring practices, ongoing awareness, annual evaluations, and recommitment events. Solution Eight contains ideas to guide the team on these efforts related to behavior standards.

While Jane and I believe that behavior standards are a

staple priority of an Employee Experience Team, each organization's team will likely have unique priorities for creating signature experience for their employees. Therefore, assessing and understanding those distinctive priorities is important work for the team.

Seeking Out Priorities

This team takes the lead on the organization's efforts to survey employees in regard to their level of satisfaction and engagement. This team conducts an annual employee survey and promotes employee participation at a high response rate. We shoot for 75 percent or higher employee participation in our partner organizations and find this to be consistently achievable.

In follow-up to the survey, the team analyzes the results and develops action plans for improving satisfaction based on the priorities identified. The team will coordinate with leadership related to communication of annual employee survey results and the resultant action plans.

Throughout the year, the team can continue to monitor employee engagement through focused mini employee surveys. The purpose of this activity is to assess the progress of the team's action plans.

The team will also want to communicate the positive impact of changes, especially those that were identified through the survey process. The team needs to "connect the dots" between the survey and the positive changes. This will promote continued employee participation and build trust in the survey process. For more information to guide the team's efforts related to survey activities, you will want to review Solution Ten.

Other tactics to seek out input for determining priorities for improvement are the use of exit interviews and stay interviews. Exit interviews allow you to understand the departing employee's perspective about their employee experience (good and bad) and what is prompting their departure. The organization will want to standardize a set of open-ended exit interview questions. This set of questions should be updated on occasion to include a key question or two that focuses on aspects of employment that have been identified as being problematic and targeted for improvement.

A face-to-face meeting is the most effective. Timing the interview a few days before the employee's last day, or even in the couple of weeks following that, often works best. As the person that is conducting the interview, you will want to do more listening than talking. You will want to avoid getting defensive when criticism about the organization is provided. You will also want to end the interview on a positive note by thanking the exiting employee for their service. Let them know that the exit interview information is helpful and wish them the best in their new venture.

A "stay interview" is a form of employee rounding. It is a proactive relationship-building conversation. Stay interviews allow an organization to explore the reasons why employees stay and what might be frustrating them in an effort to understand what may be done to make this a better place for them, and others, to work. A standard set of open-ended stay interviews should be developed, as well as a plan for when and how the interviews will be conducted. As with exit interviews, the stay interview questions should be updated on occasion to include a key question, or two, that focuses on aspects of employment that have been problematic and are being worked on.

If your organization's human resources department is already conducting exit and stay interviews, the members of the Employee Experience Team may wish to assume this organization-wide responsibility. The Employee Experience Team is focused on making the organization a great place to work and will focus their stay interview questions with the entire organization in mind. To complement the team's efforts, stay interview–type questions can be included in the questions that leaders ask when rounding. Leaders will often ask stay interview questions during rounding with their specific work units in mind.

We believe that exit and stay interviews done by a more neutral member of the organization will result in more candid feedback. When conducted by a member of the human resources department, the likely contact for future employment references, employees may not be entirely candid as a way to avoid burning any bridges. And, with the employee's direct supervisor, candid responses may be withheld in regard to any issues related to leadership concerns.

If your organization continues the process of having human resources or leaders conduct the exit and stay interviews, the Employee Experience Team should request access to the information gathered through these processes to help them in their improvement efforts.

Sample Stay Interview Questions

1. What do you look forward to when you come to work each day?

2. What keeps you working here?

3. What changes could be made to create the best job of your life?

4. Think back over the last twelve months. What frustrated you the most at work?

5. What makes for a great day at work? How often do great days happen?

6. What could be done to make this a better place to work?

7. What may tempt you to leave?

8. What are you most proud of at work?

Sample Exit Interview Questions

1. What has been enjoyable and satisfying for you in your time with us?

2. Why are you leaving?

3. The quality of supervision is important to most people at work. How was your relationship with your leader? Can you describe the positives and

negatives regarding how you and your department were managed?

4. Think back over the last twelve months of your employment here. What frustrated you the most at work?

5. Would you consider working here again in the future?

6. Would you recommend us as an employer to others? Why or why not?

7. Would you recommend our services or products to others? Why or why not?

Facilitating Improved Communication

When Jane and I assemble employee focus groups to discuss their employee experience, the topic of communication consistently rears up as an opportunity for improvement. In fact, it is often ranked as one of the top priorities to be addressed.

A very successful tactic to improve organization-wide communication is the use of a quarterly employee forum, or town hall, meeting format. One of our partner organizations calls them quarterly staff meetings. Solution Seven, which overviews tactics for improving transparency and creating systems of open communication, will provide the team with more ideas for implementing forums.

An important point to emphasize for the Employee

Experience Team is the role that employees have: in particular, the role of having key input into the agenda of each forum.

In many organizations that use an organization-wide forum for communicating to employees, the agenda is often set by senior administration. The agenda is driven by what leaders think that employees want and need to know about, when, in fact, the employees know what they want to hear about from leadership.

The Employee Experience Team can connect senior leadership with the hot topics in the workforce so that the right topics are on the agenda. Leaders are usually great communicators, but if they are speaking on the wrong topics, employees are not going to perceive this as great communication.

If the organization has a communication plan, the Employee Experience Team can play a key role in helping implement the plan. Again, often these tactics are left to leaders, even when employees are willing and able to contribute successfully toward these initiatives. The team may take on the responsibilities for a monthly employee newsletter or an employee blog or website as part of the communication plan.

Promoting Recognition, Appreciation, and Celebration

When we assess organizations, we often observe a missing element in their culture, and that is one of recognition, appreciation, and celebration. In Gallup research, weekly recognition and praise for good work is one of the twelve elements that is a predictor of employee and workgroup performance. Yet, when asking employees or teams about the last time they were rec-ognized, or an achievement or progress was celebrated, many struggle to recall the last meaningful recognition or celebration.

While leaders can make greater efforts to recognize, ap-preciate, and celebrate individuals and teams with great im-pact (more often and more sincerely), additional efforts can be spearheaded by the Employee Experience Team. In Solution Three there are many ideas to get your team going in the right direction. One particular tactic that we see Employee Experience Teams leading is employee-to-employee recognition programs. Just as coaching feedback doesn't always have to come from a leader, neither does recognition, appreciation, and celebration. These can be peer-to-peer activities.

Engaging Employees Through a Suggestion Program

As mentioned early, great organizations have high standards for behavior, performance, and contributions. Often, we fall short on engaging employees to contribute at higher levels. We know that given that opportunity, employees will amaze you with their contributions. A tactic your organization can use is to cre-ate a robust employee suggestion program. Employee sugges-tion programs can be part of your culture of contributions and an enabler on your journey to peak results.

You are certainly familiar with Post-it notes. But did you know that these were the result of an employee suggestion pro-gram at 3M? While not all employee suggestions are going to have a multi-billion-dollar impact on your organization, there is some value in most every suggestion. A suggestion may provide value to customer service, the employee experience, quality and safety, growth of services, improved workflow and efficiencies, environmental and community impact, decreased expenses, or increased revenues.

A well-designed program goes beyond the lowly suggestion box hidden in some dark corner of the organization. We encourage you to dust off this underutilized and underpromoted concept. Strive to create a program that will tap into employee ideas in an effort to improve the processes, services, and products of your organization.

Early in my career, I recall a single suggestion box with tiny slips of paper located near the cafeteria. It was hardly ever talked about and seldom was a suggestion dropped in the box. More often than not, the rare suggestion was related to the cafeteria.

To harvest the best ideas that your employees have, a well-designed employee suggestion program includes the elements of leadership support, program promotion, idea submission, idea review, idea implementation, feedback, and recognition.

Leadership Support

Leadership support includes frequent communication about the importance and impact of employee suggestions, as well as the ongoing promotion of the program. It is a topic to have on the employee forum or town hall agenda, and staff meeting agendas, on a consistent basis.

Leaders are often tapped on the shoulder to assist with the development and implementation of a change based on an employee suggestion. Leaders must respond to this. When employees' ideas fall way down on leaders' priority lists, the program will lose momentum and possibly die on the vine. You don't want to be sending a mixed message to employees along the lines of, "We value your ideas, but we don't have time to act on them." While all suggestions cannot be added to your to-do list, those that align to key strategies that are already at the top of your priority list are prime suggestions to act on.

Leadership support is needed in the way of allocating resources for idea implementation, software for idea submission and tracking, and prizes. It doesn't have to cost a lot of money, yet the processes and approvals for accessing necessary funds are part of any program.

Program Promotion

This element isn't left to leaders alone. The Employee Experience Team can be the champion promoters of the program.

Get creative about your promotion plan. You want to build enthusiasm and trust in your program. You want to create a lasting buzz. The program must have a name that is branded throughout the organization so that everyone knows what you are talking about when you mention it by name.

The promotional plan should include memorable messages that are emotionally compelling and easy to understand. Include stories about the wins and successes of the program. Be clear in your call to action. You want employees to submit ideas!

Another great promotion tactic is to include a theme and a special prize for the quarter. This keeps the promotion and the focus of the program fresh.

Examples of Themed Employee Suggestion Promotions

■ A prize of a privileged parking space to the employee who submits the best suggestion for improving the grounds, exterior, and parking lots on the campus.

■ A prize of free meals in the cafeteria for the best suggestion for improving the patient dining system.

■ A prize of paid time off for the best suggestion for reducing employee turnover.

Suggestion Submission

This needs to be made simple and quick. Employees will be intimidated and dissuaded from participating if this step is complicated and cumbersome. Many organizations still simply use a paper form for submissions while others have customized internal software or have purchased specialized software for this purpose. The Employee Experience Team members will likely be able to determine which approach is going to garner the most suggestions from employees. With a new program, starting with paper might be a great first step. Automated options can be explored as the program evolves.

The basic elements of a submission form include summary and benefits of the idea and details about the idea to the level that the employee has developed the idea. This may include details on how to implement and the projected cost. Ask a few open-ended questions then give them space to write.

You may want them to categorize their suggestion, such as checking a box indicating whether the suggestion is related to improving the customer experience, quality, safety, finance, growth, community, environment, or the employee experience. Some organizations may customize the form each time they do a promotional campaign and make the form specific to the campaign.

You will want to capture the employee's name and preferred contact method. This is great for follow-up communications with the employee, as well as recognition. You can give the option of anonymity, but this isn't highly encouraged. In some situations, an employee may elect this if they have a suggestion that is highly sensitive, such as a serious safety issue that has been unresolved through other attempts. Most likely, the desire to remain anonymous relates to public recognition. Therefore, offering the option to remain anonymous in public recognition will satisfy your employees who don't prefer publicity. Each individual's submission should be personally acknowledged as received.

A great practice we observed in one organization was the promotion of the suggestion program during the quarterly town hall meetings. A theme was selected, such as finance, service, or quality, for each town hall meeting, and suggestions were solicited from employees. We witnessed great employee participation and the results of many implemented employee suggestions.

Suggestion Review

The Employee Experience Team is a great forum for reviewing the submitted suggestions. In a well-promoted and utilized program, there will be many suggestions to review. Similar to an annual employee survey, there will be more suggestions than can be possibly implemented. Therefore, a recommendation regarding the outcome of a suggestion must be made. The decision might be to accept and implement, table and bring back for review within a certain time frame, or decline. The recommendations are often provided from the Employee Experience Team to a designated leadership group. Once a decision has been made in regard to the status of each suggestion, the submitting employee should be updated on the status.

Implementation of Suggestions

The true success of an employee suggestion program is in the actual implementation of employee ideas. An employee suggestion program will not continue on if ideas aren't implemented. When they are, employees need to know about it. The team should design a process for assigning suggestions to individual leaders, departments, or teams to own the continued development and implementation of the selected suggestions. A tracking process should be fashioned to monitor and report on the status of implementation.

Great Communication

Incorporating great communication tactics within your employee suggestion program is important for the success of your program. Some suggestions are listed below.

Program Element	*Communication Tactics*
Leadership Support	Organize CEO quarterly forums, monthly staff meetings
Active Promotion	Create Newsletters, Posters, Emails
Submission of Ideas	Acknowledge each employee who submits a suggestion
Suggestion Review and Selection	Follow up with each employee regarding the status (i.e., accepted, tabled, declined) of each suggestion and expected next steps
Implementation of Suggestions	Engage employee, if applicable, in suggestion implementation. At a minimum, keep employee up to date on the status of implementation on a scheduled basis
Recognition	Follow through with individual, organizational, and possibly even public recognition: certificates, thank you notes sent to employee homes, personal Thank You from CEO, note in personnel file, mention in newsletters, meetings, award ceremonies, etc.

Employees should be encouraged to contribute to the organization's success. While there are many ways to engage employees, a suggestion program provides all employees an opportunity to contribute ideas. This takes a well-designed program that includes the elements of leadership support, program promotion, idea submission, idea review, idea implementation, feedback and recognition, and great communication.

Creating Opportunities for Socializing and Fun

Many people spend a good portion of their lives at work, often spending more time with their coworkers than family and friends, so why shouldn't they enjoy it?

When the Employee Experience Team at one of our partner hospitals was developing their organization's behavior standards, they were emphatic about having a standard related to having fun at work. We recall the resulting discussions about the appropriateness of having too much fun in the serious environment of a hospital. Yet, the employees advocated that this was an important element in their employee experience, as well as an element that had once been there and had faded. Work had evolved into something that was no longer fun. They wanted the fun back.

If we are not paying attention to this important aspect of our employee experience, it can fade away. Yet, it's often quite easy to make any workplace fun, and it doesn't have to cost a lot of money. Someone, or a team, needs to champion this. We support the Employee Experience Team as such.

If your organization has not had such efforts organized in the past, the team may want to start slow and evolve into a regular plan of social and fun activities. The team will want to plan activities that are appropriate for the current state of the culture and evolve as the culture evolves.

This aspect of the team's work can be a lot of fun for the Employee Experience Team as well. Often the team is well suited to coordinate employee or family events and to assist with creating lower-key opportunities for elements of fun to be introduced into the workplace.

The team may help the organization celebrate recognized holidays in the workplace in fun and creative ways. In hospitals, there are always events like National Doctors' Day, Nurses' Week, and Hospital Week to be celebrated. There is also an unofficial national holiday, National Fun at Work Day, which is January 28 (but often celebrated on the last Friday in January), and National Employee Appreciation Day, which is the first Friday in March. But you don't need to wait for a national holiday to have fun at work. Get creative and have fun creating fun.

Promoting the Benefits of Working for the Organization

It is common to uncover employee dissatisfaction in specific areas such as benefits or workloads. We are not discounting that in some work environments, these concerns are very real. Yet, when conducting focus groups with employees, we often determine that these are common topics of misperception.

One of our partner healthcare organizations had this very thing happen with employee satisfaction related to their benefit program. At that time, the senior leadership and human resources professionals in the organization knew that their benefit package was on the higher, more comprehensive side when compared to employers in their community and surrounding region.

In creating an action plan to improve employee satisfaction with their benefits, a communication plan was developed to share information with employees regarding their hospital's benefit plan compared to others. An individual report could be provided to employees relaying the value of their benefit plan to show their total compensation package of wages and benefits. Without changing their benefit or compensation package, satisfaction increased as awareness increased.

Often in organizations, we have amazing benefits available to us, many of which we may not fully understand the value of, or even know about. I worked for an organization that had a very generous education-funding program. It was very underutilized and underappreciated. Why? Because employees didn't even know it existed. How many organizations have comprehensive wellness and employee assistance programs that lack participation? We see many.

An Employee Experience Team can take on the responsibility of truly understanding the many benefits of employment and promote these to employees. Also, the team can develop new programs to benefit employees.

For instance, we've seen the creation of concierge service made available to employees. In this example, the local businesses that participated supported the infrastructure of the program.

It made sense for them to do so as they benefited from increased sales in dry cleaning, car washing, and even grocery sales.

Take, for instance, the grocery sales example. One hospital arranged for a local grocery store to accept faxed grocery orders from employees with a specified pickup time. When employees left work, their grocery items were packaged at the courtesy counter awaiting their quick pickup and payment. This program, developed by the Employee Experience Team, didn't cost the hospital any money and was greatly appreciated by employees.

Promoting a Great Physical Environment

The surroundings of our workspace can also be a contributing factor in job satisfaction. We have goals to achieve peak performance in our organizations, yet if our physical environment is not attended to, we may not be inspired to rise to greatness in our work processes and interactions. In essence, our physical environment can bring us down. We recommend that the Employee Experience Team monitor for signs of this in the employee surveys, exit or stay interviews, and by conducting environmental rounds in the organization.

Environmental rounds are focused on visualizing the environment that employees work and provide services in. The team will want to create an environmental rounding plan to conduct on a routine basis, often done annually or semi-annually. The rounds often include brief interviews conducted with a sampling of employees who work in the space being evaluated. Collectively, the team then uses this information as part of their ongoing assessment, planning, and evaluation related to their team goals.

Alternative Team Models to Engage Employees

In addition to, or in place of, the Employee Experience Team we have seen success with the creation of twelve-week teams. A Twelve-Week Team is assembled similarly to the Employee Experience Team in relationship to leadership, membership, and size. The focus and time frame, however, is narrow. The team selects one or two priority actions that they can complete in a twelve-week time span. There can be one Twelve-Week Team organized at a time or multiple teams functioning concurrently.

Holding Productive Meetings

For whichever team model your department or organization adopts to improve the employee experience, you will want to conduct great meetings. Great meetings are facilitated to maximize the value of meeting time, stay focused on the team's purpose and plans, and engage team members to contribute.

How often your team meets depends on the amount of activity that needs to be organized through meetings. You don't want to meet just for the sake of meeting. There needs to be a clear purpose to meet. You want to meet often enough to keep your team engaged and inspired, and keep the progress of your team moving forward toward its goals.

In our partner healthcare organizations, their Employee Experience Teams meet for one hour on a biweekly basis for the first year and often can back off to monthly meetings after that

Employee Experience Team Agenda
Date/Time/Location

Agenda Items

Wins/Successes

Action Plan Reviewed/Updated
Agenda Topics from Action Plan:
1. Behavior Standards Monthly Focus
2. Annual Priority #1
3. Annual Priority #2

Employee Suggestion Program
1. Quarterly Theme and Promotion
2. Suggestion Review and Recommendations

Upcoming Employee Forum Planning (quarterly)
1. Date(s)/Time(s)/Location(s)
2. Attendance Promotion
3. Prepare Evaluation/Mini-Employee Satisfaction Survey
4. Other Forum logistics
   a. Meet w/CEO/Sr. Leaders for Agenda Topics

Annual Employee Engagement Survey Preparation (annually)
1. Survey Dates
2. Participation Promotion
   a. Recap of Progress based on previous year's results (e.g., Stoplight Report)
   b. Incentives
3. Other Survey logistics

Re-Cap Decisions and Action Assignments
Meeting Evaluation (ALL)
   What went well?
   What can be improved for next time?

Next Meeting:
Date/Time/Location:
Agenda Topics:

first successful year of organizing their efforts. They may need to meet on an ad hoc basis during times of peak team activity.

With a method of assignment and accountability for follow-through, a lot of team activity can be accomplished outside of meetings. The meeting purpose then focuses on collaborating on priorities and action plans, committing to action assignments, and fostering accountability for the work of the team and its members.

Well-organized team meetings include an agenda and meeting materials that are received by members in advance. A sample agenda is shown on pg. 198. Some teams include the name of the person responsible for the agenda topic as well as allotted time for each agenda item. A timekeeper is then assigned at the start of the meeting.

The team will want to develop a consistent system, such as a shared drive or email group, for meeting documents. As far as meeting minutes or notes go, the team can decide on the formality of this. Meeting notes should document priorities and action plans, action assignments, and any decisions of the team. Meeting minutes or notes are important for those members who may miss a meeting. Often, employees can start to feel disengaged from a team if they aren't updated on team happenings when they can't be there. You can avoid this with concise meeting notes that are easily accessible.

Team leaders often mention that it can be challenging, especially in the early formation of employee-populated teams, to engage employees in volunteering for action assignments that need to be completed in between meetings. This can lead to team leader burnout as they are taking on the majority of the team's work in between meetings. To assist with this, we recommend the use of Action Assignment Cards.

Employee Experience Team

Action Assignment Card

Date: __ / __ / __

I am going to contribute in this way:

Due Date:

The team can print action assignment cards on brightly colored cardstock to have available at meetings. As the leader is facilitating the meeting, they can hold up a blank action assignment card when something needs to be assigned, then ask which team member (or several if needed for the assignment) would like to be assigned. The team member accepts the card and they fill in the action assignment with the due date. The team member takes this card with them as a reminder of what they committed to do.

Or, the team leader could hand out a card to everyone at the start of the meeting and, as the meeting progresses, everyone leaves committed to doing one thing. Near the close of the meeting, each member's action assignment can be quickly reviewed and confirmed. Action assignments should be recorded in the meeting notes.

The intent is to create employee engagement in action

assignments and majority participation in meetings. When we check in on teams, we get concerned if we observe the leader of the team doing a majority of the talking. The goal is to turn this around where the employee team members are the most vocal in team meetings. We coach team leaders to be keenly aware of this and to strive to engage the team members to open up and contribute to the conversation.

Keeping Team Members Engaged

Team leaders will confide in us their concerns of having only a handful of their team members actively engaged and contributing toward the work of the team. It may be a trend of low attendance by the non-contributing members or limited participation when they do attend.

In these instances, we encourage the team leader to meet privately to understand the specific team member's barrier to engagement. On occasion, it is the lack of support from the employee's direct supervisor, an episodic or chronic situation of time pressures, or even lack of interest in the team's purpose. Don't jump to conclusions about a team member's lack of engagement or participation. Take time to meet with them, understand their issue, and work toward a personalized resolution.

Call to Action

The engagement of employees in a team effort to improve the employee experience can be a major contributor in the endeavor to achieve peak performance.

If you currently have a team designated with this purpose, consider some of the ideas in this solution to refresh and re-inspire your team. If your organization doesn't have a team, consider championing this initiative in your organization or in your department. The following Employee Experience Team Success Plan can serve as a guide through this process.

The Employee Experience Team Success Plan

Evaluate Current State

- Is there an organization-wide team, functioning as an Employee Experience Team, committed to this purpose? Is it employee populated? Are there clear priorities and action plans developed? What are the major activities assigned to this team? Is the team successful in their efforts?

- Are there other teams in the organization committed to this purpose? Are they employee populated? Are there clear priorities and action plans developed? What are the major activities assigned? Are they successful in their efforts? Are efforts across teams well coordinated?

- If there are no such teams in your organization or department, is there support for creating a team? Conduct key stakeholder interviews with human resources, senior leaders, peers, and employees to gauge interest.

Plan and Make Improvements—
Select and Prioritize Based on Assessment

If there are no employee experience teams in your organization or department:

- Champion the creation of an organization-wide team (or department team if current lack of support or ability to create organization-wide team) with clearly defined purpose of improving the employee experience.

- Solicit team members who meet recommended qualifications.

- Engage team in assessment activities leading to two to three priorities for the year.

- Engage team in activities aligned with identified priorities.

If employee experience teams exist but are not organization-wide:

- Champion the expansion of the efforts to an organization-wide team with clearly defined purpose of improving the overall employee experience.

If an organization-wide Employee Experience Team exists currently:

- Champion the continuation and expansion of the team's efforts utilizing tactics provided within this solution.

Evaluate and Adjust

- Regularly reassess to evaluate if the team efforts are leading to improvements. Adjust plan and team activities as necessary. See Solution Twelve for additional guidance.

Transparent Communication

Communicate unto the other person
that which you would want him
to communicate unto you
if your positions were reversed.
—Aaron Goldman

When Sue and I enter an organization for the first time to assess their work culture, we often hear from employees that they perceive communication to be poor in their work environment.

We meet with groups of employees and ask them to describe what the very best work environment would be like. Invariably, the employees respond along the lines of "better communication from the top down and across all of the departments." They then clarify with comments like "no one tells us anything" and "everything is a secret around here."

Then we will meet with the senior leadership team of the very same organization, on the very same day. Those leaders will share with us that one of their strengths is communication. Hmm.

What leaders may not consider is that communication is more than talking. Communication comes in many forms, and being an organization that communicates well takes planning and, of course, behavior change.

Transparency in communication takes a dedication to being open to sharing all that is happening in the internal workings of your organization, as well as the external environment that is affecting the work that your employees do.

It may take a concerted effort to recognize that your employees are adult professionals who deserve the opportunity to form their own opinion on what is happening in their organization.

Sue and I worked with a leadership team that was hesitant to pass on information about their financial status to their employees. We assessed that employees were very concerned about the organization's finances. Yet, the leadership stance was, "We do not think our employees are ready for this. We don't think they will understand it." Ironically, their financial status was actually good news! Not only should they have communicated, but they should have celebrated with their employees.

This solution will focus on the benefits of an open, transparent communication plan, as well as some best practices that Sue and I have come across over the years.

When taking into consideration the vast amount of communication you play a part of on a daily basis, you may come to the conclusion that you are a master. Practice makes perfect, right?

Well, if filling up the air around you with words makes you an expert communicator, I am a PhD and deserve a lifelong tenure at a top university.

Your words as a leader are very important. Your words are

weighed and measured as soon as they come out of your mouth. Your words are heard over and over again in the minds of your employees as they consider what the words meant to them.

Frequency in communication is good. I spent the early part of my career just communicating everything. I had learned that you cannot overcommunicate. That is not necessarily true. If you inundate your employees with emails and read from meeting minutes out loud at a staff meeting, they are soon just going to tune you out.

Your communication style is uniquely yours. However, as with everything else in leadership, it takes thoughtful consideration.

Your communication style, philosophy, and competency will impact the *trust factor* of the words that are said. Developing an open, transparent communication style that results in the trust factor being extremely high is one of the most important skills a leader can hone. It makes everything else a leader may do much, much easier.

Communication without trust is just words in the air. Remember how the famous cartoon character Charlie Brown's teacher communicated to them? "Blah, blah, blah, blah, blah." You don't want this to be how employees view messages from leadership.

When you consider that frontline leaders are the communication connection between individual departments and the entire organization, the trust factor in frontline leadership is just as vital as that of senior leadership. An organization without trust, at any level, is paralyzed.

When there is limited trust between departments, leaders, and employees, it is as though there are invisible walls put up between everyone who works there. It is a natural human experience and reaction that when an event happens that is perceived negatively in an organization, those employees who have no trust build a wall around themselves. Soon, everyone starts protecting his or her own real estate. They are afraid they will suffer loss as well. Anxiety starts to run very, very high. Organization focus is limited, maybe even nonexistent, as self-preservation and protection become the center of attention.

Something I lived through in one of my first leadership jobs taught me a tough lesson on communication and trust.

I encountered my first employee termination meeting. Firing an employee is never an easy or fun activity. This employee, Matthew, was a very well-liked member of my team. He had been my peer prior to my promotion to a leadership position.

I worked in a large organization that had well-defined protocols for terminating employment. At the conclusion of the termination meeting, I was told by the human resources administrator that firing Matthew was strictly confidential and I could discuss it with no one.

My limited leadership knowledge and experience and the lack of ability to think clearly in this highly emotional situation are the only excuses I could give for what I did next. I returned from the human resources department back to my department after having been gone for several hours. When I had left the department, I had left with a fellow employee. He was not with me on my return, and another employee had been assigned to complete his shift.

Everyone was staring at me as I walked past into my office, closed the door, and stayed in there, never even coming out for water or coffee. For hours. In my own defense, I was likely fighting a war within myself, knowing the right thing to do was to have a team huddle and let the employees know that Matthew would not be working in our department any longer but that I could not share the details with them. I could encourage them to support Matthew in any way they felt they could or should.

I, of course, did not do this.

Soon, one of the employees stormed into my office and slammed the door. She stood there, facing me with her hands on her hips. Her words were not in search of her missing friend and colleague. Her words were, "What the hell is going on around here? Who else are you going to fire? Does this mean all of our jobs could be snuffed out at a moment's notice?"

Whoa. I quickly became defensive and told her I could not talk to her about it.

It took me a long time to rebuild the trust I lost that day. It didn't need to happen that way if I had been thoughtful and considerate of how my employees must have felt, not just about Matthew, but about their own jobs. I mean, what did I think my team was going to assume? That Matthew had been abducted by aliens?

My employees began to put up walls and created silos. They did this naturally to protect themselves and their livelihood. What was created was a natural slowdown of progress. Basic leadership tasks such as scheduling became more difficult. Finding new employees to fill Matthew's position or other vacant positions in my department became challenging. We no longer could have employee-involved discussions about things like cost-saving measures. Defenses were up most of the time.

Delivering Bad News

Leaders will need to convey bad news sometimes. It may seem like it is often. Leaders must give careful consideration each time. As trust is built over a history of open and transparent communication, employees will likely accept bad news without it adding fear and anxiety to their lives and their jobs. You won't lose momentum in the progress being made toward achievement of the goals and strategies.

Sue and I learned another lesson about delivering bad news when we encountered a team of senior leaders' missteps in delivering news of a pay cut that affected all employees and leaders. On the same day this news was communicated across the entire organization, the senior leaders were nowhere to be found! One had sent out an email saying he was unavailable for two weeks on a cruise! Another posted pictures on Facebook the same day of a sunny place that she had just flown to. The last senior leader left in the place had given strict orders to his assistant that he was working on a project and could not be disturbed. He even had a window shade temporarily hung over the window of his closed office door so that no one could see if he was in his office.

"So sorry for your luck! You should have had a savings account to live off of." That is the message all of those employees received right along with the pay cut news.

Do not leave for the day or make yourself unaccessible as if the bad news meant nothing to you! Be present. Be mindful of the negative impact bad news could have. Make sure to respond to fear and anxiety, no matter how irrational you may think it is.

As difficult as it is to convey bad news, it is vital that you do it. To *not* bring up the elephant in the room is to make the elephant bigger. If you do not share with your employees in an open and transparent manner, you give permission for the rumor mill and grapevine to rule. If you do not tell employees the truth, they will fear the worst. And when communication is absent, employees will make up their own version of the truth!

Walk the Talk

When leaders do not communicate openly and transparently in order to build trust, the walls and silos that are formed can drag progress to a grinding halt.

An organization without trust built from transparent communication is one in which a leader may have to jump through ten hoops to get a policy passed because leaders do not trust each other to advocate for the right things.

An organization without trust built from transparent communication can take months to hire a new employee because the human resources department cannot trust that leaders will follow the steps to select the right candidate.

Trust building from transparent communication also requires "walking the talk." Acknowledge here and now that you are in the spotlight as a leader, and your actions speak as loudly as your words. Conversely, you can choose to feel as though the spotlight of leadership is actually a microscope, and you can freely express yourself without consequence.

The clearer reality is that leaders *are* on the big stage. One example of being "on stage" but "not walking the talk" is when a

CEO openly stated that he believes in open communication and transparency; yet he was infamous for not responding promptly, or at all, to emails or messages from employees or other leaders.

Or the example of a hospital leadership team that openly declares that improving financial strength and patient satisfaction are the highest organizational priorities; yet, the team overspends on lavish furnishings and art for the new wing of administrative office suites. All the while, the patient care unit was denied new mattresses for the patient beds in that year's capital budgeting process.

Do you see how mistakes such as these could call integrity and trust into question? In this regard, I have an algebra equation for you to consider for leadership: *Integrity + Trust = Relationships + Results.*

The book by Stephen M. R. Covey, *The Speed of Trust,* is a great read on creating a culture of trust. In this book, Covey describes thirteen trust behaviors. Two of these behaviors are commitment and accountability.

Covey refers to commitment as the "Big Kahuna" of all the trust behaviors. When you make a commitment, you build hope. When you keep a commitment, you build trust. Be careful when making commitments. Make only the commitments you can keep. Also, don't be vague when making commitments.

In a 2002 Golin/Harris poll, "assuming personal responsibility and accountability" was ranked as the second-highest factor in building trust. Great leaders build trust by first holding themselves accountable then holding others accountable.

Holding yourself accountable includes taking responsibility for bad results. It is often our natural response to blame others for failure. When we fail, we need to look in the mirror. I was at fault for the lack of trust in my leadership that resulted when I fired Matthew all those years ago. I should have stood up for my leadership values of open communication and transparency when another leader told me I could not say a word to my team.

> **Trust is like the air we breathe. When it's present, nobody notices. When it is absent, everybody notices.**
> —*Warren Buffet*

Trust is part of the invisible architecture that is present in your building. It is more important than the bricks and mortar that hold the building up!

Communication Practices at the Department or Work Unit Level

Leaders are busy. Yet, employees are busy too. Employees need to know where to go for certain information. They need to know how to shuffle through all of the emails they get from *everyone* in the organization to get the information they need.

My employees were always telling me that they received too many emails. When they would admit that they had missed an important email communication from me, I would selfishly say "Well, read my emails first!" This was the wrong way to go about it. I needed to triage communication by labeling the priority of the message in the subject line of the email, or devise another system for communicating priority information.

The leadership tactic that gives you the biggest bang for your buck in open, transparent communication is rounding. The most effective and powerful communication is the one-on-one conversation. So simple, yet so effective. When you engage in rounding conversations, when you follow up and follow through on what you discover, it is a trust builder. It is also a way for you to be seen as approachable for future conversations. Round every day you work, and never give it up. It is too important.

Another tactic is to practice consistent methods of communicating information. Having a communication plan you follow, and that your employees know about because they helped develop it, is worth the effort.

A communication plan needs to build consistency, yet the methods need to be diverse. Employees have their unique preferences as to how they best receive information. You cannot expect your twenty-something millennials to respond to the same communication techniques as your baby boomers. So, a variety of communication methods are needed within the plan.

The plan often focuses on methods for group communications to employees, yet some leadership consideration must be given to planning for the individual's preferences when a leader needs one-on-one communication. This may be as simple as how does the monthly schedule get communicated to all employees compared to how does each employees have their unique preferences as to how they want to receive information. There may be some special considerations that need to be made if you have employees working "off-shifts" or scattered across multiple buildings, or in some businesses, employees located around the globe.

In approaching the development of a communication plan,

engage the employees. You can ask the question about communication preferences during rounding. You can hold special employee meetings with a special focus on communication preferences.

Once input is gathered on how employees prefer to receive open and transparent communications, then proceed to consider the *types* of information that will be communicated.

Is this a safety issue that needs to be conveyed immediately? The plan should spell out how employees will consistently learn of urgent issues. Are there things they need to know before they start their work for the day? This could be delivered in a preshift huddle, or an email with a special title in the subject line, or a specific message board designated only for this purpose.

Is the organization going through some changes and there may be lay-offs? If your department or organization size allows, the plan will likely call for a direct personal communication, such as an impromptu meeting, so that questions can be answered and information discussed.

News about new employee benefits, changes to the cafeteria menu, and an update on an organization-wide project may be delivered in a newsletter format that is hosted on an employee webpage. Employees can print it or access it online to read at their leisure at work or at home.

For time sensitive communications sent via email, state clearly in the subject line "Please read prior to XX-XX-XX, important information about XYZ."

Consider the use of posted communications. Bulletin boards in employee lounges or high-traffic areas and space near the time clock often work effectively. In my past, our communication plan called for posting information at the time clock that was important to read before the start of the shift. Some time clocks even have the ability to convey a message when your employees punch in.

Sample Department Communication Plan

1. Non-urgent communications, including the minutes of the weekly senior leadership team meetings, will be in the form of a weekly newsletter which can be accessed on the employee web page. Read within one week of publication.

2. Need to know today: *emergent* communication means live and in person. The leader will seek out all who need to know to deliver the message individually or in groups.

3. Weekly and non-urgently means a weekly newsletter on the employee web page. Print or read online within one week of publication.

4. Biweekly reporting of all goal metrics will be posted on the department's goal board.

5. The monthly schedule will be posted four weeks in advance in the online scheduling system. Employees are required to review the new schedule prior to the start of the schedule. Changes to the schedule after posting will be communicated via phone call or direct communication.

6. Monthly and routine conveying of updates and results will be conveyed in the monthly staff meeting. Meeting notes will be posted on the department's bulletin board within 24 hours of the meeting. Those who were not in attendance at the meeting must read the posted meeting notes within one week of the meeting date. The employee will sign and date the posted notes to indicate they have read the information.

7. Quarterly updates to goal action plans will be posted on the department's goal board.

8. All emails will have a clear subject line, including response date for time sensitive communications.

9. The leader's blog will be published biweekly with goal updates and important department and organization-wide communications.

Soon after implementing and adhering to a communication plan, your employees will no longer believe rumors. They will trust that you are going to bring the good, the bad, and the ugly to them in a timely fashion they can rely on. Employees that do not dwell on rumors or gossip are more productive and engaged!

Beyond the elements of a systematic communication plan, another component of open and transparent communication with employees involves the annual performance evaluation and day-to-day performance feedback conversations. When I say "timely" I am referring to the rules of your organization for when performance evaluations or conversations are to be held. When employees know the rules, they feel anxiety and distrust when something does not happen as it should. Make sure you get these conversations completed in a timely fashion. If you cannot, explain why, not just to human resources or a senior leader, but also to your employees.

Solution Two expands greatly on the topic of day-to-day performance feedback conversations, or direct dialogue. Putting direct dialogue into use in your day will aid in your open and transparent communication efforts.

Bulletin boards have been posted in workplaces forever with papers strewn all over them. Put these boards to great use by making them an effective communication tool that simply cannot be ignored in your workplace. These should be hung in a prominent place in your department. Post communication on the board in a balanced approach. In healthcare, we suggest the headings of Finance, Growth, Quality, People, Service, and Community be displayed. These headings certainly can be amended to make sense for other types of organizations.

Do not hide bad results from your employees. Make sure they are posted, with an action plan, and a follow-up discussion at a staff meeting or a special meeting. Make sure, as well, that a lot of positive things are posted on the board.

If your senior leadership team publishes their team meeting minutes, which Sue and I strongly encourage for transparency sake, make sure these are posted on the communication board or distributed in a timely fashion. Employees love reading what goes on at the "big" table!

Another great tactic for improving communication

through the use of bulletin boards is to start each huddle or staff meeting at the communication board. We are big fans of "standing meetings" anyway. We know of organizations who consistently engage in this practice and note employee and leader satisfaction with this new routine. One organization we work with conducts its monthly Board of Trustees meeting in this fashion. Give it a try and see the benefits.

Warning: do not post a conference announcement involving a cruise ship if you have no intention of sending an employee there.

Department goals and results need a prominent place on your communication board. Employees want to trust that their efforts are producing results and that they work for an organization that keeps track. I often heard from my employees that they "like knowing that we can come to work and see how we have been doing on our goals." Keep the board updated weekly or biweekly, or at least monthly. If you cannot get to this, delegate it to an employee who has the dedication and creativity to do it well.

Communication Practices at the Organization Level

As was introduced in the prior solution, Solution Six — The Employee Experience Team, creating a quarterly employee forum event is a powerful communication tactic. These forums take on different names in the different organizations, but the purpose is the same. The objective is to directly communicate important information about the status of the organization and its efforts to achieve its key strategies. The CEO of the organization is often the one addressing the employees at the forum, yet sometimes other senior executives may be involved.

Instead of a one-way communication like reading an email, forums are a way for discussion to happen; liken it to FaceTime with the CEO. I have seen some organizations make it work with the senior leadership teams taking turns to facilitate these forums. However, I do not recommend this unless the CEO absolutely cannot be effective with this form of communication. I have come to appreciate that the voice of the CEO is very important to employees. The CEO's voice commands respect and communicates the vision for the organization in a way that others often cannot, no matter how brilliant or articulate the other leaders may be.

To achieve the most from employee forums, we recommend that you engage the assistance of the Employee Experience Team, or some equivalent of employee involvement in planning and preparation. In larger organizations such as those with more than fifty employees, or those with multiple offices, buildings, or campuses, forums will have to be repeated over multiple offerings to reach a large audience of employees. In this regard, the Employee Experience Team can advise on the number of forums, the times of days, and the location of forums.

Sue and I also recommend that the development of each forum's agenda is a collaborative process with the Employee Experience Team or equivalent. Some agenda topics will be of the CEO or senior leadership team's choosing. Not all, however. It is vital to the success of your open and transparent communication that employees also weigh in on the agenda topics for the CEO to address. Your employees truly know what drums are beating in the jungle of your organization! They know what employees are wondering or worrying about. These items can be transparently addressed at the forums.

An example of this played out in one organization that I worked for in the past. When the employee team met with the CEO to devise the upcoming forum agenda, the employees were very clear with him that he needed to keep them abreast of an employee who had embezzled several thousand dollars from the organization over a period of years. This organization was in a small town, and the employees wanted to know, "Why is she still out in the community? Why hasn't she gone to jail yet? What are we doing to make sure this never happens again?"

Of course employees wanted to know that. This request should have come as no surprise to the CEO. Their organization had been robbed. For employees with a high degree of loyalty and trust, this is like their own house being robbed. So bless this CEO, he talked about the crime and the trial at each quarterly forum until it was not an issue anymore. This calmed the gossip on this topic, as employees knew where to get answers.

Another very effective method of communication for CEOs is a monthly written update which is emailed or posted on an employee website. I have stressed that systematic and purposeful communication is key to being an open and transparent communicator. That same CEO who discussed the embezzlement case every quarter for years also did an amazing job of sending out monthly CEO updates to his employees. They arrived in a broadcasted email to all employees on the first of the month at midnight, no matter what. No matter what golf tournament, vacation, holiday, or financial disaster was happening, his employees could count on that.

The message is always in the same format. It is purposeful and systematic. The typical format includes growth or decline in volumes, the status of major building or renovation projects, the current results of customer satisfaction and quality reviews, and whatever is on the minds of employees that he learns through rounding documentation or meeting with employees. Long or short, it is there every month. Employees look for it. They know they can rely on him. Frontline leaders can adopt this too.

Call to Action

Whether you lead a small or large organization or a work unit within, all leaders can engage in tactics to improve communication. Sue and I have yet to encounter an organization in which employees have boasted that communication was perfect and there were no opportunities to improve. So it's likely that there are some opportunities to improve communication in your organization. And in some organizations, hopefully not yours, where severe distrust levels exist and where secrecy abounds, it requires a big call to action for positive change.

Whatever level of need that you may face, I hope that within this solution you have gained some pearls to improve the employee experience related to open and transparent communication. Great communication can seem like an intimidating ideal, and it's not uncommon to feel overwhelmed. Don't let that stop you.

As with any improvement, narrow the focus. Consider one, or at most a few, tactics that may assist in your efforts. Then, just start. And when you are ready for more, move on to another tactic or two. Customize these tactics to make them yours, and soon your employees will be saying what an amazing communicator you are!

Open and Transparent Communication Success Plan

Evaluate Current State

- Seek out any documents that relate to communication protocols or plans in your workplace. Look at handbooks, policies, and communication plans.

- Review applicable employee survey results looking for strengths and opportunities related to communication and trust. What opportunities for improvement are identified? Are there identifiable pockets of strength in communication in certain departments or work units?

- Review your written communication. Assess your last ten emails or other forms of written communication to employees. Assess if email was the most effective approach. Was it a clear, concise, and transparent email communication?

- Reflect on your personal communication efforts in the past year. Reflect on the positives that have resulted. Reflect on the struggles that are present. Consider if your communication approaches are consistent, systematic, and effective. How effective are you at communicating in staff meetings or other types of meetings? Is there a trend of gossip or a strong rumor mill? Do employees approach you for information or discussions? Do you "walk the talk?"

- Review posted communications or other prominent methods currently utilized. What are the strengths and weaknesses? Are they open and transparent? Is the information timely? Is it being received by employees?

- Round with employees and peers with the specific intent of gathering feedback on the current state of communication and trust, as well as communication preferences and suggestions.

Plan and Make Improvements—
Select and Prioritize Based on Assessment

- Develop or revise a communication plan in keeping with the assessment findings.

- Engage employees in executing the communication plan. This can include employee involvement in the communication board, recording staff meeting minutes, or the creation and distribution of a newsletter.

- Seek out opportunities daily to provide feedback on behavior, performance, and contributions. Keep in mind the guidance of the three-to-one compliments to criticism ratio and generational preferences in regard to feedback that were discussed in Solutions Four and Five.

- **Organization Change Agent:** Advocate for an organization-wide adoption of a policy for transparency and open communication and an applicable communication plan, including employee forums and other senior leader communication strategies.

Evaluate and Adjust

- Regularly reassess to evaluate if the changes are leading to improvements. Refer back to the assessment activities above to guide the reassessment. Adjust plan and improvement activities as necessary. See Solution Twelve for additional guidance.

Behavior
Standards

Behavior is a fickle mechanism. Being at the head of this grand clockwork, attempting to understand its nuances so that you may promote its well-being can be a monumental task. Yet time and time again in our work with organizations that want to achieve peak performance, we are faced with implementing change related to behaviors. And *behavior change is hard.*

It is a privilege, not a right, to work in our organizations. With that privilege comes responsibility, or what could be considered conditions, of our employment. These responsibilities call for us to *behave, perform,* and *contribute*. In organizations striving to achieve great results, the standards for behavior, performance, and contribution must be set high. Everyone must not just accept them but strive to achieve these high standards.

When working with organizations that are creating a strategy to achieve greatness, we often do an exercise in which we ask groups of employees and leaders to describe what their organizations would look like in a "wildly successful" state. In follow-up, we ask them to then list the specific actions of employees and leaders that will move the organization to this new place of being "wildly successful."

Oftentimes, this exercise results in many of the participants calling for similar action. Though there are always exceptions, the common thread that runs through each and every action plan involves changes in behaviors. Employees intuitively know that behaviors in the workplace have an impact — good or bad.

Bad behaviors in the workplace can cause everyone, not just the target of those behaviors, to lose motivation, engagement, and loyalty. When an environment of bad behavior is fostered, employees may stop caring about quality, service, growth, finances, or productivity. In essence, they lose the will to contribute to the overall success of the organization.

Bad behaviors are costly in more than just the metaphysical realms. Staff turnover, decreased productivity, absenteeism, and underachievement can almost always be tied back to bad behaviors gumming up the gears. The American Psychological Association reported in 2010 an estimate that bad behaviors cost businesses $300 billion annually.

When it comes to behavior, what we accept is what we teach.
What we permit, we promote.
What we allow will continue.

The benefits of a civil, safe work environment where high standards are defined and upheld far outweigh any opposition to such a notion. Benefits such as improved work communication and relationships; enhanced decision-making, innovation, and learning; engaged, motivated, and loyal employees; reduced turnover and absenteeism; increased productivity; and improved quality and service will ultimately lead to peak performance and the achievement of organizational goals.

To aid this monumental effort to improve behavior, performance, and contributions, we always recommend that high standards be clearly spelled out in a set of behavior standards. These behavior standards should be developed by your employees who already embody the ideal of great behavior.

Gone are the days when standards are unwritten rules that possibly only the old guard seems to remember. Gone are the days when employees argue over interpretation of these unwritten rules, citing changing times as an excuse for poor behavior. Behavior standards should be the model for all daily actions by everyone in the organization, from top to bottom.

Sample Behavior Standards

- I will give customers priority over all personal interactions.

- I will identify and report safety and quality concerns promptly and apply remedies whenever needed.

- I will communicate with courtesy, clarity, and care in all verbal and nonverbal messages.

- I will always be open to give help, ask for help, and accept help.

- I will acknowledge customer dissatisfaction, apologize for the situation, and strive to remedy the situation. If I am unable to remedy the situation, I will find someone who can.

- I will keep others informed and explain delays, changes, or altered expectations.

It is imperative that once behavior standards are articulated, everyone in the organization commits to these high standards and holds each other accountable to them. This isn't a situation in which organizations rely on some trickle-down effect from leaders to employees; it's also about peer-to-peer accountability. The hope is that all can embrace the standards as adults and, in this embrace, find it within themselves to hold one another accountable for their behaviors and actions.

It is far too easy to fall prey to the negatives when speaking on behavior standards. We love promoting the idea that these new standards come alive in a positive manner, meaning that positivity and recognition will occur three times more than any coaching or constructive activities surrounding them.

Behavior standards need to be kept alive by relentless focus upon them. The documentation of these standards cannot be relegated to a bin or dusty shelf; it must be kept vibrant and alive in employee minds, creating the new normal of "this is how we do it around here."

Recently, we were working at one of our partner health-care organizations that had developed their behavior standards two years before. We encountered the example of an interaction between a student from a local university and a phlebotomist. On the student's first day with the organization, the phlebotomist had this to say to the student: "We are rated number one in the state of Michigan for patient satisfaction. We have behavior standards that spell out how we treat each other and our customers. We want to stay number one, so everyone, including students, must follow these standards."

Now, there is an organization in which behavior standards are alive and well!

This solution will focus on providing information on developing and utilizing behavior standards as an organizational tactic for improving results. While we encourage the entire organization to develop and be held to clearly defined standards, sometimes that is just not in the logistical cards. If this is the case, applying behavior standards to your personal span of control can be the spark that lights the proverbial flame. Once you start achieving excellent results with these new standards, others in your organization will take note. Once they do, the rest of the organization will no doubt begin to make an effort.

Creating Behavior Standards

Unless you just cut the ribbon on a new organization, developing behavior standards is not a "start from scratch" procedure. From our experience, we see that most healthcare organizations, and likely most other businesses, have a Code of Conduct that resembles behavior standards.

We often observe that these documents have some common problematic themes:

- They tend to spell out "what not to do."

- If they are used at all by leaders, it is usually in a punitive manner.

- They are most likely created by leadership, not employees.

- They are "not alive," meaning that most in the organization may not be familiar with the document or the standards held within them. That said, the document is in no way guiding the day-to-day behavior, performance, or contribution of the organization's employees.

As a starting point on the path toward developing behavior standards, we ask the organization to assemble a team of employees to develop the standards. If the organization has, or is developing, an Employee Experience Team (as described in Solution Six), we recommend that this team be responsible for developing behavior standards. If no such team exists in your department or organization, use the guidelines in Solution Six to assemble an ad hoc team that can develop the behavior standards.

Keep in mind that the team should be composed of employees who are already modeling behaviors that are positive in your work environment. This team is not a place in which employees learn good behaviors but are already shining beacons of great behaviors.

Once you have your team assembled, encourage them to seek out and review existing documentation on behavior standards for the organization. Once found, the team will then have to decide: Are we revising? Are we co-opting? Or are we throwing it all out and starting from scratch?

We have seen teams engage in a plethora of creative activities in developing their individual standards. Two simple exercises we recommend:

Exercise #1: Start by understanding the current behaviors:

- List the best behaviors you've seen at work.

- List the worst behaviors you've seen at work.

Exercise #2: Start envisioning a new and better future:

- Describe what "wildly successful" looks like (in your department or organization).

- Describe the specific actions necessary to achieve "wildly successful."

The information and discussions brought about in these two exercises is often enough to get the ball rolling for the team members and their development of behavior standards.

Tips for Developing Behavior Standards

1. Behavior standards should be simply stated, easily understandable by all, and specific.

2. Behavior standards define how we *want* our people to behave. Work rules, not behavior standards, are the place to define how we *don't want* our people to behave.

3. Do not create a standard for something that you are not going to hold people accountable for. It is far better to have no standard for behavior than to have a standard that won't be upheld.

4. Try to include only what your team deems as the most important behaviors needed to move the organization forward. Include too much and the behavior standards may begin to read like a textbook.

5. The behavior standards should focus on important elements such as quality, service, people, growth, finances, research, community, and other elements that accurately represent the breadth of your organization's or department's focus.

Utilizing Behavior Standards as a Key Tactic for Success

Once you have finished defining the behavior standards, commemorate and solidify the process by holding an event. Take this time to make sure that everyone reviews and commits to the new standards as a symbolic step on your way to a new culture. Jane and I always recommend that the leaders commit to the behavior standards first, starting with the most senior leader, such as the president or CEO.

This event marks only the beginning of the journey.

Efforts must be made to bring the standards to life across the organization or department and to keep them alive. Your Employee Experience Team can be the champion of this endeavor. Whatever team is chosen for the task would benefit from creating an annual plan to provide awareness reminders regarding the behavior standards. We have also seen some teams develop an annual recommitment event to accompany their plan to help keep the standards alive.

This team should also be charged with initiating campaigns for behavior standards that require more effort to reach the high level of compliance required or that are known to be most problematic in the work environment. In our travels, we have seen successful examples of "positivity" and "gossip be gone" campaigns championed by Employee Experience Teams in an effort to emphasize standards that were problematic in their work culture.

We can't stress enough how important it is to reinforce behavior standards in a positive way. To keep them alive and kicking, leaders must recognize employees who consistently uphold the behavior standards. What is recognized most often gets repeated. As mentioned before, Jane and I promote the "compliments to criticism ratio" of three-to-one. When applying this ratio, the leader's positive communication with employees regarding the behavior standards would be three times more frequent than any coaching or corrective conversations.

It may seem trite in the early phases of "bringing standards alive" to have to recognize some very basic behaviors. However, if the employees developed standards for these behaviors, they consider them necessary to achieving great results.

For instance, one organization has a standard that all employees make eye contact and extend a friendly greeting to each other as well as customers. This seems like basic, common-sense behavior. Yet it may not be commonly practiced. So as the leader, you may have to praise your employees for engaging in this behavior. Recognizing employees for seemingly common-sense behaviors is often the starting point to improving culture.

An organization we worked with to set and achieve high standards of behavior struggled with the concept of bringing their behavior standards alive in a positive way. It was historically a culture in which leader accountability equated to punitive actions. Changing to a culture in which leaders embraced positive reinforcement and positive coaching proved difficult. Very tenured leaders would need to change their own behavior and approaches to employee accountability.

In the initial adoption of the newly developed behavior standards, those leadership behaviors had not changed yet. This led to too much emphasis being placed on corrective or disciplinary actions related to violations of the behavior standards and very little emphasis on praise and recognition for those who were achieving the newly defined high standards. Employees started seeing the new behavior standards, created by employees, as being a new "stick" for leaders. It took a very intentional focus on frequent positive feedback from leaders to overcome this view of the new behavior standards.

As with all endeavors dealing with individual behaviors contributing to the whole, there are going to be individuals who struggle more than others to uphold the high standards that have been set for your organization. As leaders, we need to be diligent in the coaching and corrective activities of behaviors, performances, and contributions that fall below the defined standards (Solution Two provided guidance on coaching and corrective conversations).

At the start of this initiative, you may also have to face up to negative behaviors that have been tolerated in the organization for a very long time. In starting this journey in a unionized environment, I recall a union official stating, "You've allowed the dogs to crap on the rug for fifteen years. Do you really think they are going to stop now because there is a behavior standard that says they can't?" *Yes, this is often what organizations are up against.*

In essence, an organization that adopts behavior standards is indeed saying, "It is a new day!" The past is the past. And the future is going to be much better if we all uphold the behavior standards. The highest performing and behaving employees will be thankful for a work environment in which bad behaviors are no longer ignored and higher standards of behavior are promoted.

To assist leaders in holding individuals accountable to the new standards, we recommend that the behavior standards be referred to in the work rules and be subject to the formal discipline process. They should also become part of, or be referenced in, union contracts, if applicable. Jane and I also recommend that the behavior standards be scored elements on annual performance evaluations and that self-evaluations be conducted annually. We have also begun to see an increase in the use of peer evaluations, which includes feedback on performance and behavior, as an additional accountability tactic.

When I was the senior leader and Jane worked for me as a frontline leader, I would be responsible to conduct her annual performance evaluation, which included the evaluation of her compliance with the behavior standards. She would do a self-evaluation on the behavior standards, and I would evaluate her compliance as well. Then, we would engage in a discussion of how our perceptions compared. I give her credit that she was so honest in her self-evaluation. In particular, Jane struggled (and still does) with the use of sarcasm. While sarcasm is often funny, it isn't always appropriate or in keeping with our organization's behavior standards.

The real goal in all this is to see the behavior standards become a natural extension of the culture of your organization. The more leaders that engage in recognition and coaching, the more employees will learn to engage in this same manner with their peers. Instead of only leader-to-employee accountability, the culture will evolve into employee-to-employee accountability in regard to the behavior standards.

You'll know that this is happening when you begin to see employees praising each other and "calling each other out" in reference to the behavior standards. Certainly, this "calling each other out" activity may cause some friction at first; yet, this is a sign of a positive cultural change that has begun blossoming in your organization. You will feel it, and your results will be showing it.

In many organizations, we have seen the use of a logo or symbol, often developed by the Employee Experience Team, which is posted throughout the organization, as well as worn on the uniforms of employees. This symbol provides a constant visual reminder, as well as a tool for employees to use in employee-to-employee accountability.

We also recommend the use of behavior standards as

part of the application process. Having applicants review and commit to the behavior standards prior to being interviewed cements the expectation firmly in their minds, making the organization's commitment to excellence a positive first impression. An applicant's willingness to sign the behavior standards (or not, as the case may be) can be a significant insight into their mind set and future behavior.

Bear in mind that behavior standards can also be incorporated into your interviewing process. In Solution Four, we advise on the use of behavioral interviewing techniques.

While behavior standards are developed to provide a high benchmark for behavior, performance, and contribution from the individuals within the organization, we often find that a specific department or unit is struggling to uphold certain standards.

We experienced an example of this with a food and nutrition department. After reviewing the survey data and results from employee focus groups, it was clear that improvement was being seen across the entire organization, with one exception. Though all the employees and leaders had reviewed and signed the behavior standards during the organization-wide conception, it was clear that these standards had fallen stagnant in this one department.

To get this department on the path to improvement, an intervention was organized. A mandatory meeting of all of the department's employees included the CEO, vice president, human resources director, union leaders, and the food and nutrition department leaders. The session overviewed:

1. The results of the department compared to the results

of other departments in the organization.

2. The behavior standards and the "why" behind them.

3. Identification of the problematic behaviors in the department.

4. A recommitment of each individual to uphold the subset of behavior standards that were identified as most problematic.

An example of this department's specific recommitment can be found in Appendix 7.

While a team, such as an Employee Experience Team, may have an important role in developing the behavior standards and bringing them to life, all leaders have work to do as well to aid in this effort. A simple way that department leaders can keep behavior standards on everyone's mind is to discuss them regularly. Some leaders focus on one behavior standard each and every month. They include it on the monthly staff meeting agenda. They post it on their communication board. The team starts their daily shift huddle recognizing examples of this behavior.

To decide which behavior standards are priorities to focus on, leaders can use a simple exercise on a quarterly or biannual basis. Simply distribute a copy of the behavior standards and ask employees to list two or three behavior standards that are always followed by the employee, in the department, and in the organization. They might be different in each column, as the employee may have consistently upheld standards that others in the department or organization may not. Then have the employees list the two or three behavior standards that aren't being upheld on a consistent basis. Again, they may be different for the employee, the department, and the organization.

	Me	*My Department*	*Organization*
Great Behaviors that Always Happen			
Behaviors that Need to Improve			

Celebrate those behavior standards in which there is the most agreement among employees that those behaviors are always happening. Then, for the behaviors that need to improve, plan activities to create awareness and better compliance. Seek opportunities to provide positive and coaching feedback consistently surrounding these specifically identified behaviors, remembering the three-to-one ratio.

Call to Action

A standards-based employee experience can serve as a powerful and constant sign of the organization's cultural values surrounding peak performance.

We all recognize that poor behavior in the workplace can

cause employees to lose engagement and motivation. Organizations *must* and *can* counter this by developing high standards and accountability systems. The employee-driven process to develop behavior standards and the planned organized activities to bring them alive serve as key tactics to improve results and establish a culture of success and positivity.

Take the time to assess the current practices surrounding behavior standards in your department or organization. Identify the opportunities to take these practices to greater levels, producing excellent results for your organization.

The following Behavior Standards Success Plan can serve as a guide through the discovery process.

Behavior Standards Success Plan

Evaluate Current State

- Seek out any documents that relate to standards of behavior, performance, or contributions. Look at work rules, handbooks, policies, code of conduct, vision and values statements, etc.

- Evaluate your employees' personnel files. Do they reflect information on levels of behavior, performance, and contributions?

- Is there an existing team that can develop new (or revised) behavior standards or does a new one need to be assembled?

▦ Identify the most problematic behaviors in your department or organization. Identify the most favorable behaviors as well. The use of employee focus groups and employee survey data can aid in this assessment.

Plan and Make Improvements— Select and Prioritize Based on Assessment

▦ Engage a team of employees to develop high standards of behavior. Enlist the Key Tactics for Success to commit to them, bring them alive, and keep them alive as a positive force toward peak performance.

▦ Evaluate all future employee satisfaction or engagement survey data and comments in regard to the high standards for behaviors, performance, and contributions. With employee involvement, create an action plan each year to improve adherence to the high standards.

▦ Complete annual performance evaluations, utilizing leader and employee self-evaluations of the behavior standards. Conduct these in a fair and timely manner.

▦ Seek out opportunities daily to provide feedback on behavior, performance, and contributions. Keep in mind the guidance of the three-to-one compliments-to criticism-ratio.

▦ **Organization Change Agent:** Advocate for organization-wide behavior standards that are developed by employees, committed to by everyone, and part of the selection process and the annual evaluation process.

Evaluate and Adjust

- Regularly reassess to evaluate if the changes are leading to improvements. Adjust plan and improvement activities as necessary. See Solution Twelve for further guidance.

Leader and Employee Development

An investment in knowledge always pays the best interest.
—Benjamin Franklin

An investment in your future. Money in the bank. The early bird gets the worm. Every cliché statement ever created about taking initiative to avoid disappointment, all pointing to one inalienable fact: you get back what you put in.

This has never been truer than when considering the training and development of leaders and employees.

Sue and I speak to many leaders from organizations across the country. At least once a week, we hear, "We just don't have the funds to do any training at this time."

At the very same time, she and I are present in organizations across the country, personally witnessing the waste that still happens within. These wasted dollars could be allocated to training and development. And in these same organizations, we encounter senior leaders with high expectations that their employees will achieve peak performance, yet there are limited resources allocated to develop them.

Limited resources are a reality, in healthcare and otherwise. And what we have come to learn is that leader and employee development can be achieved affordably in today's tight economy.

The reason why organizations should invest in leader and employee development is simple. Knowledge is power. A component of engaging a workforce is increasing their knowledge of the key strategies of the organization. Focusing on the skills that are necessary to achieve the organization's overall strategic plan creates the power to carry out the mission and vision.

What you are doing when you begin a development plan for your employees and leaders is teaching them to fish. Instead of feeding them by communicating the same messages over and over, begin providing and imparting knowledge that they can use to feed themselves, not only for the week or month, but over a career.

When Sue and I spent two days training leaders from a large hospital system, one of the leaders, Patrice, wrote this comment on her evaluation. "This has been chicken soup for the leader's soul. I am so happy to work for an organization that invests in me in this way."

At this particular training, the leaders experienced something amazing. They realized they were all in the same boat, frantically paddling upstream. Yet, they learned, in two days, that they have each other to rely on. Instead of being in their own silos, experiencing the chaos of the whirlwind each and every day, they learned they are a team of brilliant people who can learn together and take that knowledge to work together to create peak performance.

There were forty leaders in the room and by the end of day one, they looked at each other as if they had never seen each other before. They had not. They were so used to just going in and out of mindless meetings together, they never really stopped to consider ways they could rely on each other and coordinate their efforts. They learned more than what Sue and I were teaching that day. They learned they had a team of leaders to carry out a mission. They were not alone.

I agree with Patrice. Learning together creates a synergy that is therapy for a leader's soul.

What if we invest in training and developing leaders and employees and then they leave? That's a great question, but here is a better one: "What if we don't invest in them and they stay?"

Leaders and employees come from all walks of life. In order to get everyone on the bus and heading in the same direction, it takes training.

Training needs can be identified for specific individuals or groups within the organization. Likewise, training needs can be identified that should be consistently met for all leaders and all employees in the organization. This solution will focus on the latter.

Consistency without High Cost

The guidance that Sue and I provide to organizations is to create a consistent rhythm of training and development. This consistency provides a sense of trust and speaks to a commitment to the value of continual growth and development.

Our partner organizations conduct quarterly, off-site education for their leaders in an all-day session. They also provide organization-wide employee training sessions that are held at least twice annually.

When you begin to consider the cost of off-site, quarterly training for leaders, you're probably thinking, "That is too costly. We simply cannot afford it." You simply can't afford *not* to provide leadership development in today's challenging and ever-turbulent changing leadership environment. It likely can be done for less than one percent of your overall budget.

In many hospitals, we discover that the funding for an impactful leader-training plan can be less that the cost of the maintenance contract on one piece of high-tech radiology equipment. If you are not a leader in healthcare, consider another key piece of equipment central to your business. Is it the espresso machine at Starbucks? The brown trucks at UPS? What are your maintenance costs of operating machinery? What are you saying to your leaders if you do not spend as much money maintaining them as you do a piece of equipment?

Having an employee and leader development plan takes thoughtful consideration of the return on investment for any training. Striving to keep costs low and benefits high can be challenging. Here are some suggestions for how to make it happen.

Likely, there is a low-cost venue that will hold all of your leaders in one room. Somewhere in your town, there is a church, and that church has a basement. Rent it, and if there is not a rental fee, make a donation to the church. If the audiovisual technology is not the best there, bring your own.

Maybe the chairs are not comfy and cushy. Make it fun. Have leaders bring their own pillows or cushions for their seats and give a prize for creativeness.

For food, ask leaders to bring a dish to pass around. On occasion, provide a simple catered meal. Maybe once a year, in mild weather, have an outside training day with a barbeque.

A leadership development team can take these ideas, coupled with additional guidance in the remainder of this solution, to deliver high-quality, cost-effective leadership training. This team needs thinkers *and* doers on it. Many times, teams get nowhere with a plan because there are too many brilliant, perfectionist ruminators on it. You will need logistics people who are going to negotiate the best price for a speaker and pester everyone to bring a dish to pass to ensure that nourishment happens throughout the day of learning.

You can provide inspirational leadership development and invest in the future of your organization without breaking the bank.

Training Topics

You may be thinking, what are we going to teach leaders and employees in all of those sessions? We have never known of an organization to run out of topics to teach. We know of organizations who have conducted ten years of quarterly leadership trainings with no signs of running out of important curriculums to put in front of their leaders as they continue on with this commitment.

Most often, the easiest form of education is to teach the "tasks" associated with someone's essential job functions. Many organizations we see across the country have this type of education down pat, yet that is where leader and employee development often stops.

The missing link to the success of most organizations is imparting that strategic knowledge and linking it to necessary skills. Teach leaders and employees what they need to know and do to contribute to the organization's key strategic goals, and let them go to work in a new and more meaningful way!

For many years, the hospital that Sue and I worked for had an annual finance goal to increase profit. As part of the leadership and employee development plan, training was organized to increase everyone's knowledge and skills related to what factors impact profit. And then there came a point in which the organization's annual finance goal was changed to increasing days cash on hand. The leadership and employee finance training had to be amended greatly after we adopted this new goal. While we had all become very skilled at increasing profit and improving our income statement, we had a lot to learn about impacting cash and the balance sheet.

Ridiculous as it may seem, sometimes you have to instruct on behavior expectations. It can be challenging to teach leaders and employees on how to behave in certain situations, or how to have direct dialogue to create a better work experience. Be mindful that training to tasks versus training to behaviors such as customer service may take some different avenues of training.

There are so many training topics that will assist your employees and leaders both at home and in the workplace. For instance, teaching a communication topic like direct dialogue and

empowering employees to take care of problems and issues with
coworkers at the lowest possible level. Not only could this add
years to your life as a leader when employees handle issues on
their own, but think what it may mean to employees' home lives.

We noticed that in many organizations, training topics on
work-life balance, wellness, and resiliency are highly valued by
employees and leaders. For these types of agenda topics, make
sure in your planning that there is a clear learning objective in
regard to "what is in it for the employee," not just "what is in it
for the organization."

We knew of an organization that consistently included
a wellness topic at each leader or employee training session for
several years. However, the objective that was communicated
was that the organization wanted to reduce its health insurance
premiums by providing this employee education. This wasn't the
message employees wanted to hear. This message didn't motivate
employees to learn and make changes. They wanted to know that
their organization was committed to providing training on this
topic because they truly cared about their health and wellness.

Maybe in your organization, you already have lots of
training going on. With some careful assessment, though, you
may find that the organization needs to stop or change up some
of the current training efforts. Look at what you're already doing and see what is possibly unnecessary training or training
that is being done because "we have always done it this way."

At one point in my career when I worked as a frontline
employee, the organization kept adding to the annual mandatory training requirements. The list of required trainings grew

longer and longer. This evolved into a less than impactful, and almost frustrating, system of employee development.

Take time to conduct an analysis of what could be done in a more efficient and effective manner or dropped altogether. Make sure you are not adding to your overtime budget, or training dollars, when some education is old and needs to go away or be done in a more streamlined fashion.

Trainers and Teachers

When you determine what your employee-level and leader-level training plans will be, there are some basic expectations to say aloud when it comes to who will conduct training. This can be in policy format, if that is the culture of your organization.

The first expectation needs to be that for any training that employees or leaders attend, they will share that knowledge with others. Any investment in training must lead to sharing upon return to the workplace. This sharing could be a short presentation at a leader or employee meeting or an in-depth training workshop at the next leader development event. Sue and I find that attendees will be sure to listen and engage in one of our public training Summits when they know they need to present to the rest of the leadership team when they get home!

While Sue and I support leaders receiving training and education outside of the organization, we promote that the majority of this should be conducted internally, to the benefit of many versus a few. Outside training can be very costly; therefore, the number of people attending is often limited. We recommend that a portion of those training dollars be shifted to support an internal development program.

In this regard, Sue and I both advocate for developing "leaders as teachers and champions." While this can help to offset the cost of outside trainers and speakers, it also develops internal experts and resources.

In considering what topics might be benefited by creating internal training champions, look to the required leadership competencies. For instance, these competencies may be project management, time and priority management, and LEAN or other process improvement methodologies. Then seek out those internally with passion for these topics and invest in their development, and they, in return, can develop others.

Internal trainers can also be developed to champion employee training. I worked with a nursing leader named Jan. She had always wanted to be a "True Colors" trainer. She had a vision for how effective employees and leaders could be if they understood how best to interact. In other words, Jan was ahead of her time in wanting to know what made each and every employee "tick."

Jan was chosen as the nurse of the year, an honor that also included scholarship money for training. She used that money to become certified as a True Colors trainer. She then volunteered to teach all of the hospital's leaders and employees what she had learned.

Jan is a bright, engaging leader anyway, but when she taught our leaders how to interact with each other and collaborate as a team, and then taught hundreds of employee members how to do the very same thing, the positive impact spread like wildfire through our organization.

All of this resulted from an investment in training a passionate champion. You have people like Jan in your organization. Watch for them, then engage them and develop them! Never underestimate the power of one impassioned leader, whether they hold the title of leader or not. One person can make a difference. Just as one person can weigh an organization down with a toxic attitude, another can light a fire under the organization with passion, energy, and training.

There certainly are occasions in which outside trainers or speakers are beneficial. Our experience is that leaders and employees truly enjoy the diversity of a training event that includes internal and external trainers.

Keep costs low by looking around your community, at a local college or university, or at a vendor that may offer free or low-cost training on the topics important to your development plan.

If you decide to invest from time to time in an expensive external trainer, a great tactic is to partner with other businesses in your community that also desire this same training. Or, you could do what a small community hospital does. Once a year, they organize a community-wide training on improving customer service or the employee experience. While all of the hospital employees and leaders are benefiting from this training, so are their family members, friends, and others in the community. The organization is seen as a community leader and a great place to work through this example of investing in training, not only for their own employees, but also for the community.

Creating a Leadership Development Plan

A comprehensive leadership development plan takes into account three main factors: leaders' identified learning needs, the organization's priority goals and strategies, and the required competencies of all leaders.

The starting point of creating a plan for leadership development is to conduct a learning needs assessment. Appendix 8 provides an example of one that Sue and I have used for many years. In our partner organizations, this assessment is completed every two years. In between those intervals, a thorough training evaluation at the conclusion of each leadership training session provides an opportunity for leaders to weigh in on their leadership development needs. Design a development plan that includes the priority learning needs identified by the leaders, remembering that there needs to be something in it for them.

Additionally, the organization must determine what learning needs exist in relation to the established strategies and goals. If the organization has a priority strategy to improve customer service, the development plan should address this topic. If days cash on hand is your finance goal for the year, leaders will need training on what this means and how best to achieve it. Leaders will need to reach an understanding on how their department can help to achieve the overall goal.

To create additional emphasis on the organization's key strategies and goals, a best practice we recommend is for the

CEO to open each leadership development session with an update on the key organizational results. This update provides opportunities for recognition and celebration. Or, if some results are not trending favorably to meet the established goal, the adjustments to the action plan can be shared.

We advise, however, that leadership training does not devolve into information sharing. This can be accomplished in other forums. In preparation for your training curriculum, assess that the agenda includes a majority of true development versus informational content. Otherwise, your trainings will soon be perceived as just a really long meeting.

Sue and I see examples of organizations that have clearly defined leadership competencies and a development plan to strengthen those competencies. On the other hand, we also see organizations that haven't given leadership competencies much thought.

In our partner organizations, we work with them to adopt a leadership framework that guides the identification of competencies. These become important components in the leadership development plan. For instance, these competencies may be hiring and evaluation, talent management, communication, goal setting and action planning, financial analysis, or quality improvement methodologies.

With these identified learning needs, goals, strategies, and leadership competencies in mind, steps to developing a leadership development plan include those listed below.

Steps for Developing a Leadership Development Plan

1. Conduct a leadership learning needs assessment every two years.

2. At each leadership training offered, all leaders complete a comprehensive evaluation which goes beyond simply evaluating the training and includes questions such as, "What other leadership development needs do you have? What other topics for trainings would you like to see?"

3. Identify the organization's priority strategies and goals set for the year.

4. Consider the competencies required of all leaders.

5. In preparation for the upcoming year, draft the curriculum and objectives for each quarterly training session. Refinements and adjustments can be made to this plan as each leadership training event approaches.

6. Set the dates for quarterly leadership development prior to the start of the year. Communicate these dates to all leaders, getting them placed on the leaders' schedules well in advance. The CEO needs to make sure he or she communicates that these

trainings are essential for the organization's success and are therefore mandatory. Our recommendation is that only the CEO can excuse a leader from attending a mandatory quarterly training.

Sue and I promote that leadership and employee development is a "Learn, Do; Learn, Do" cycle. For each training event, we suggest that a learning roadmap, call-to-action plan, or follow-up "to-do" list be developed and provided to each attendee. Providing it at the start of the training allows the learners to focus throughout the training on what is expected of them after the training. The attendees will know that they are trusted and empowered to go forth and carry out what they have learned. An example of a learning roadmap is shown in Appendix 9.

As you move down the path of consistent leadership training in this fashion, you will need to develop a plan for "catching up" your newest leaders. It will hit you one day that these new leaders missed out on the benefit of all the past quarterly leadership trainings.

An organization could take the sole approach of orienting new leaders to these topics individually. Yet, an approach that Sue and I promote is creating a New Leader Training Series. This training series could be offered at various intervals throughout the year, based on the volume of new leaders. While leaders still have a component of orientation to the key topics selected for this training series, new leaders would also learn together in a didactic-type group training series. This is where your internal champions that you have created over time provide additional value by assisting in the training of new, or emerging, leaders.

Creating an Employee Development Plan

When Sue and I led at an organization that developed an organization-wide training plan, we made a grave mistake in the first three years of our efforts. Initially, the organization's development plan only focused on training leaders. Though unspoken, we expected our leaders to go back and teach their employees the skills that applied to them. Some of the leaders did that effectively, but not every leader did.

What we learned is that inconsistent and optional training leads to inconsistent and optional results. We had been transparently communicating the results we were getting to the employee level, but again, magically assuming they would know how to help us or that the individual leaders would make that happen.

The light bulb was turned on when our Employee Experience Team brought forward a recommendation for the creation of an employee development plan. They recognized the need for a plan to bring the employees on the bus and get them rocking and rolling down the road with us. This team knew that a consistent and systematic process for organization-wide training was an important part of the answer. At that point, an Employee Training Team was formed. Leader led, yet employee driven like the Employee Experience Team, this new team was charged to create and execute the organization's annual employee development plan.

We began a plan to educate employees on our goals and strategies and the skills and behaviors needed by all to achieve these. As mentioned before, sometimes you need to be very direct and specific in your training approach regarding the expected standards of behavior. Employees may perceive that they are giving great customer service, when in reality there is opportunity to learn and improve. Getting specific through high-quality training can aid in these efforts.

I recall teaching employees a customer service technique that was simply saying "hi" in the hallway and taking patients and visitors where they needed to go in our building. Often, I would get a blank look from employees in the audience. They were likely thinking, "Duh, lady. I am always friendly. I say hi to everyone in the hallway every day." I would then point out to them that I walked down a hallway to get to the classroom or auditorium and that a rare few had said hello to me.

Training can be the start of a new day, creating a heightened understanding of the high standards required to achieve peak performance. Leaders and employees have likely been walking down the same hallway, staring at the floor, walls, or worse, *a cell phone*, for years. It takes practice to carry out amazing customer service techniques. In follow-up to training, employees were encouraged to self-evaluate every day, and try to do better the next day.

What we learned is that employees needed to be taught, and they needed to be taught all together with different departments interacting together to achieve the same synergy that our leadership development events did. Our employee training sessions were much shorter, only two to four hours in length, and repeated many times over several days to promote high attendance. And this has been going on two to three times per year for many years, and it continues today, in this organization.

Our employee development was not deemed mandatory. That said, a healthcare organization that we partner with has created a system of mandatory employee training three times a year. This hospital has achieved the number-one ranking in patient satisfaction in the state of Michigan for two consecutive years. They strongly believe that training is an important tactic leading to their success.

When we began taking our employees on the journey with us, our results skyrocketed. Don't leave your employees behind. Break your organization's annual goals down, and determine what employees need to learn so they can contribute, and then teach them to fish!

Call to Action

Your first steps may be to get organized or reorganized to create a consistent and high-quality plan for training leaders and employees. If you belong to an organization that has a department responsible for employee and leader training, such as an education or organizational development department, this is an amazing resource.

Even given that resource, it is important to engage key stakeholders (i.e., the leaders and employees working throughout the organization) to contribute in the plan's development and execution. We caution against creating a silo-type education or organizational development department. These types of departments are service or support departments for the entire organization. Just like financial success can't happen with only the finance department's efforts, the same is true of training.

Create an organized rhythm to the annual training schedule. Leader and employee training events are in a sense "branded" within the organization. When anyone sees or hears an announcement of a leader or employee training event, they all know exactly what to expect. You want to create positive branding around the organization's training efforts. You know you've got a problem if training becomes dreaded.

Make sure that the development you are providing is fulfilling, not sucking everyone's emotional bank account dry. If all you do is preach at your leaders and employees during a supposed development opportunity, they are really not going to want to continue attending.

Also, if the perception is that there are a ton of extra to-dos in follow-up to the training, development sessions will be dreaded for this reason as well. I heard leaders in an organization say once, "Spending a day away from our desks makes us have to work that much harder when we get back." Yes, leaders and employees should have new tactics to try out when returning from training, yet this should not be overwhelming. Hence the recommendation for quarterly leadership training versus all at once, one time per year.

Think balance. What does the organization need to get out of the session, and what does the learner want to get out of the session? Keep it in balance.

Treat leader and employee development like a change

management and continual improvement project. The Success

Plan below can guide in these efforts.

The return on investment may not be immediate. Yet, over time the investment may last a lifetime for your organization.

Leader and Employee Development Success Plan

Evaluate Current State

■ Conduct a comprehensive overview of the current *employee* training activities. What training activities are centralized? Which are decentralized? What resources are allocated? What activities are focused on organization-wide development needs? What are the strengths and weaknesses? Who is responsible for organization-wide employee training? Are the training topics in alignment with the organization's priority goals and strategies? Do the training topics consider the required competencies and behavior standards? Are trainings evaluated and the feedback received used for improvements and future training needs?

■ Conduct a comprehensive overview of the current *leadership* development activities. What training activities are centralized? Which are decentralized? What resources are allocated? What activities are focused on organization-wide development needs?

What are the strengths and weaknesses? Who is responsible for organization-wide leader training? Are the training topics in alignment with the organization's priority goals and strategies? Do the training topics consider the required leadership competencies, behavior standards, and group-identified learning needs? Are trainings evaluated and the feedback received used for improvements and future training needs?

- Assess leadership and employee learning needs. Conduct a leadership learning needs assessment. Assess the need for work-life balance training by interviewing a representative of your occupational health or wellness team or department.

Plan and Make Improvements— Select and Prioritize Based on Assessment

- Create recommendations, based on your assessment, to improve the *employee* training activities.

- Create recommendations, based on your assessment, to improve the *leadership* training activities.

Evaluate and Adjust Plan

- Evaluate each training session. Use the feedback to plan and make continual improvement. Communicate to leaders and employees the changes and improvements that were made based on their input.

- Regularly reassess to evaluate if the leadership and employee training efforts are leading to improvements in your organization's results. Adjust the plan as necessary. See Solution Twelve for additional guidance.

Surveying and Improving the Employee Experience

When we only trust our gut in regard to the current status of the employee experience, we may not be armed with the knowledge needed to initiate, or continue, the drive to improve.

I have a personal example in which I relied on subjective information to guide my health and fitness goal. At the hospital where I worked, the organization had adopted a key strategy of improving employee health and wellness. I jumped on board and was engaged in improving my health. I changed my diet and joined a healthy lunch club at work. I exercised daily for sixty to ninety minutes.

I had been on this plan for nearly two years when I attended an employee wellness fair to have laboratory tests completed. These lab results led me to understand that my action plan for improving my health was not complete and that I was not reaching a goal of better health. I had a laboratory value that was critically wrong. Burst my bubble! How can this be? I felt great. I'd been eating right and exercising.

Yet, the reality was that I needed a new action plan, which included surgery, to make a correction to this finding. If this lab data had not been brought to my attention, I would have continued to subjectively believe that, "I haven't felt better in my adult life, and my plan to be healthy is working perfectly."

We can find data like my surprising lab result in regard to the health of our organization's employee experience. And, just like a routine wellness checkup, we should be monitoring important data on a regular basis. Armed with this, we will have information to evaluate the effectiveness of our action plans and point us in the direction of further improvements.

Jane and I recommend that organizations utilize an annual survey process to gather information about the current state of the employee experience. This solution will be filled with our insights from many years of working with organizations to conduct and utilize such surveys to the benefit of their employees. Even if your organization is already using a survey process, within this solution you will likely find some ways to enhance your current process.

By itself, a survey does not improve the employee experience, just as a lab result doesn't improve your health. A well-designed process of surveying, reporting, goal setting, action planning, and accountability can be a catalyst for positive change.

A Well-Designed Survey

When organizations are on the path to gathering survey data on the employee experience, a decision needs to be made as to whether the survey will be designed and administered in-house, or if an outside vendor will be utilized. The benefits to taking the internal route are often cost savings and a bit more control over the survey timing and distribution method. The downsides can be the lack of access to expertise related to the survey questions, the validity of the survey, choice of distribution methods, a perceived lack of confidentiality, data compilation, and interpretation.

Also, with an internal survey process, organizations lack the ability to compare their data to others, removing the ability to benchmark their results. Jane and I also observe that organizations often underestimate the time and resources needed to administer a high-quality internal survey process.

Whether internally developed or with the assistance of an experienced survey vendor, the survey must be well designed to harvest the needed feedback on the key elements of the employee experience. It is like ordering the correct laboratory tests to measure my health on an annual basis. Collect the wrong lab results and I may not know the true picture of my health.

When in the process of selecting a vendor, you will likely come across various types of employee surveys. Some vendors may conduct an Employee Opinion Survey, which focuses the survey questions on employees' views, attitudes, and perceptions of the organization. Other vendors may survey for Employee Engagement in a process that is designed to measure commitment, motivation, sense of purpose, and passion. Another common survey is an Employee Culture Survey, which measures the shared assumptions and beliefs from the employees' points of view. Our preference is a survey that measures opinions, engagement, *and* culture.

You will want to select, or design, a survey that takes less than fifteen minutes for an employee to complete. You can usually evaluate up to seventy or eighty elements in this amount of time.

One of our partner healthcare organizations asks less than ten survey questions but does this each quarter. They have picked questions that relate to the key drivers of employee engagement and regularly update their action plans with the feedback they receive on this quarterly survey.

If you utilize a vendor experienced in employee surveying, they will likely have pre-set survey questions or a list to choose from to customize your survey. With vendors, pre-set questions are often necessary if you want to gain the ability to benchmark your results to others.

When developing your own survey or working with a vendor to customize your survey, you will want to include questions that focus on employee perceptions related to various aspects of their work environment, their interactions with their coworkers and leaders, the new employee experience, the culture of safety and quality, and any perceived learning or development needs.

Tips for Selecting or Developing a Great Survey Tool

- Include personalized survey elements. These elements start with "I" or "My."

  □ "I know what is expected of me."

- □ "I am committed to the achievement of our goals."

- □ "My workload is manageable."

- Avoid vague items or terms and jargon that employees may misunderstand or misinterpret.

- Survey about employees' perceptions of coworkers, direct supervisors, and senior leaders.

- Avoid evaluating two or more items in a single statement.

  - □ "I have the equipment, supplies, and training I need to do my best work."

  - □ If the element is scored low, you cannot decipher where the opportunity for improvement lies. Is it in equipment and supplies, or is the opportunity in training?

- Avoid adding words that qualify the statement, such as "usually" or "often."

  - □ "My coworkers are usually committed to doing quality work."

  - □ Leave the "usually" out and the rating scale will be more helpful.

- Place survey questions randomly throughout the survey; avoid grouping like items.

- Ask question about overall satisfaction and engagement.

  - "I consider myself a satisfied (or engaged) employee."

  - "I plan to continue working here for the next year or longer."

  - "I would recommend this company as a great place to work."

  - "I am proud to work here."

- Ask questions about the culture of safety and customer service. These can be utilized in organization-wide, as well as department-specific, safety and service improvement efforts.

- Ask questions about high standards of behavior, performance, and contributions.

- Ask identifiers (e.g., length of employment, work unit/department, age/generation, level of position). We recommend the first two as a minimum given the helpfulness of these identifiers in the analysis and planning process.

- Utilize a five-point Likert scale for the response.

- Allow for comments related to each element.

- Ask some open-ended survey questions regarding employee and patient safety, customer service, and training needs.

In regard to surveying the culture of safety, we know that some healthcare organizations already survey this separately from the employee experience survey. If your organization does not, we highly recommend that it be added to the annual employee survey. Adding an open-ended question or a mandatory comment section related to safety concerns or suggestions is also very helpful in the organization's improvement plans. Some organizations also include open-ended questions to harvest ideas for further employee training and development and customer service improvements.

Consistency of your survey questions over time is advised. If you are frequently changing vendors or survey questions, you lose the ability to trend your results over time to monitor for changes. There may be some slight changes in the survey from year to year, but complete overhauls result in the loss of your historical trends. In essence, you are starting over with new baseline measurements. At certain points in the organization the benefits of changing your survey may outweigh the downsides. However, careful consideration should be given.

Some of our favorite employee survey statements are listed in Appendix 10.

Another key element in a well-designed survey is the rating scale. Jane and I are fans of utilizing a five-point Likert scale, and we find that this is most commonly used by survey vendors.

An example of common wording and the corresponding points used in calculating a score for each element for a five-point Likert scale are shown below.

1 = Strongly Disagree, Very Poor, Strongly Dissatisfied (0 points)

2 = Disagree, Poor, Dissatisfied (25 points)

3 = Neutral Fair (50 points)

4 = Agree, Good, Satisfied (75 points)

5 = Strongly Agree, Very Good, Strongly Satisfied (100 points)

We have seen some organization-developed surveys in which a four-point scale is used by taking out the option to select a "neutral" response. This is in an attempt to have employees commit to being either satisfied or dissatisfied (or agree or disagree). While we prefer the five-point Likert scale, if organizations use another scale, it is recommended that they use it consistently in their series of surveys so that they can have comparable results. Later in this solution, we will cover more on the topic of analyzing the results with the scale that is chosen.

High Survey Response Rate

We challenge each of our partner organizations to achieve a high response rate on each employee survey. The goal is to have 75 percent (or more) of the organization's employees complete the survey, and we have seen this goal met or exceeded a majority of the time. Yet, we have also known of organizations getting far less than half of their employees to participate in the survey process. This section will include best practices that will help your organization garner high employee participation.

An initial communication from the CEO is a good way to announce the upcoming survey. A CEO-delivered message conveys to employees that this is an important process. This communication should emphasize that the survey is a tool to aid employees and leaders in making the organization a great place to work. The emphasis in this communication is that past surveys have resulted in improvements and this upcoming survey will too. Employees want to know that their time and input is not wasted.

Next, engage your Employee Experience Team and all leaders, including union leaders when applicable, to promote the survey. The Employee Experience Team and leaders can detail some of the positive changes from the input gathered in the past survey and promote the promise of future changes based on the input received. The aim is to create broad commitment and buy-in to the benefits of the survey, while at the same time not overpromising that every issue identified in the survey can be addressed before the next survey. Promote the promise that priority issues will be identified and improved and that employees will be involved in these activities.

The Employee Experience Team and leaders may organize incentives or contests to promote participation. Small incentives are commonly used. One of our partner healthcare organizations is known for their amazing no-bake cookies sold in the cafeteria. They are a rare treat that many employees enjoy. The Employee Experience Team worked with the cafeteria to provide no-bake cookies to employees upon proof of completing the survey.

In other organizations we have seen departments challenge one another to see which one can get to 100 percent completion first. Some have offered a prize drawing entry to each employee who completes the survey in the defined early bird period (i.e., the first few days of the survey).

A great way for leaders to promote the survey is in one-on-one discussions with their employees. They could simply add a question to their daily employee rounding such as, "As you know, we are conducting our annual employee experience survey. Have you completed the survey yet?"

If the employee hasn't, the leader simply asks, "Are there any questions I can answer about the survey or in any way assist you in completing the survey?"

I know many leaders who routinely approach employees and offer to take over their workload for the fifteen minutes necessary for the employee to complete the survey.

Some may feel that protecting anonymity of the responder is important in a high response rate. In some cultures with trust issues, this may be a valid concern to be addressed in the administration of the survey. Yet, over time, as the culture of the organization improves, we see anonymity as a non-issue in the design and administration of the survey.

While you don't have to collect employee names or too many identifiers on the survey, at a minimum you should know which department or work unit the respondents work in. Therefore, some of the promotion around the survey participation should be related to participants correctly identifying their department or work unit. In very small work units, the survey design may group like units together in some fashion to assist with concerns of anonymity. Employees need to know how to correctly identify their department or work unit when they complete the survey.

It is also recommended that someone be designated to monitor and report response rates by department throughout the survey period. Jane and I have often seen this done successfully through the use of a large display in a public area. This visual keeps employees up-to-date on the survey response rate.

A survey period of two to three weeks is often long enough to achieve a very high response rate. In some organizations, the survey is offered in both electronic and paper formats to assist those employees who aren't so computer savvy. We are seeing the use of paper surveys diminishing as computer usage increases. This is helpful too as the electronic format is often more cost effective when it comes to data entry and compilation.

Initiate Activities Surrounding Survey Results

Once the survey has been administered, you are faced with lots of data and comments. A benefit of an experienced survey vendor is their expertise in compiling, analyzing, reporting, and benchmarking. Organization-wide results, coupled with work unit (i.e., department, unit, division, etc.) results, are the most helpful in setting goals and developing and monitoring improvement plans.

We have encountered organizations that did not have department-specific survey results. This becomes challenging when trying to develop the most appropriate improvement plans. In one of our partner healthcare organizations, they began administering their annual employee surveying with only organization-level results for a period of two years. They achieved overall organizational improvement in those two years.

Then, starting in their third year of surveying, they began collecting department-specific results. While the overall organization-level results showed more improvement, they were now able to clearly see in the department-specific data where the biggest opportunities existed for future action plans in departments with very low satisfaction results.

In another partner healthcare organization, they had historically collected department-specific survey data and comments. This turned out to be quite helpful when we noticed very low overall scores in the elements of new employee orientation and onboarding. From the overall organization-level scores, it may have been easy to jump to the conclusion that an organization-wide overhaul needed to happen to their orientation and onboarding processes.

The department-specific results were able to identify only three departments that had very low results, while the majority of departments had extremely high satisfaction in these elements. Thus, the action to overhaul the entire organization's processes was not necessary. The appropriate plan was for the low-scoring departments to apply the processes that already existed and were being successfully used by the majority of the departments.

We recommend that all leaders and members of the Employee Experience Team review the data, comments, and reports in preparation for optimal use of the survey findings. Reviewing and analyzing results may be accomplished in a session in which a representative from the vendor or designated internal person facilitates.

The objective of this session is to make sure that the results are understood, that key trends are identified, that comments are reviewed to aid in a clearer understanding of the data, and that comparatives to any benchmarks are analyzed. This same session, or separate follow-up sessions, should be focused on setting the organization's annual goal and preparing for the organization-wide and department-specific communication and use of the results.

Prior to a work session of the leaders and the Employee Experience Team, it may be helpful to get the compiled reports in the hands of the session attendees prior to the event. To prompt review and preparation for these work sessions, a worksheet could be utilized to guide their preparation for the meeting. An example is in Appendix 11.

When analyzing the data, we are often drawn to the survey elements that received the lowest score or have the highest number of dissatisfied or strongly dissatisfied responses. These may be, indeed, the areas that are your highest priorities for improvement. We challenge leaders to look at where they received the lowest number of the "top box" response as well.

The appropriate place to improve may not be in your lowest scoring elements but may be the survey elements in which the response to the highest possible rating (i.e., strongly agree, very good, very satisfied, etc.) is very low. In these incidences, you may see a pretty high overall score. This is often because the response to the second highest score (i.e., agree, good, or satisfied) is very high. Often, our biggest opportunities to improve lie in the elements in which we are "good," and we need to create plans to turn these into "very good" responses.

When we focus our attention on the low volume of very poor or poor responses (and the comments that accompany them), we often aren't prioritizing the opportunities to make improvements that affect the majority of our employees. *Good is the enemy of great,* which is why we recommend that you *focus on turning your "good" to "very good."*

It is also tempting when compiling and reviewing data to combine favorable responses. For example, combining "good" and "very good" together to report the affirmative responses of employee engagement. While indeed both responses are positive, there is definitely a difference in the level of satisfaction and engagement of employees who will select a rating of "good" versus "very good." The behavior of your employees, as in their willingness to expend discretionary effort or recommend the organization as a great place to work, can vary based on their rating of "good" or "very good."

By comparison, if you go to a new restaurant in town and you rate the food, service, and experience as "good," you may or may not go there again, you may or may not recommend them to others, and you may or may not talk positively about this restaurant to others. However, if you rate that dining experience as "very good," it is a good bet you will go there again, recommend it to others, and talk positively about it to others.

We want our employees to have a great experience, one that they will recommend to others, talk positively about, and demonstrate their loyalty and commitment to.

In summary, we should go beyond focusing on only our lowest scores and hone in on the lowest percentage of top-box responses. Beyond the scores, how much focus should be placed on the comments? Jane and I recommend that you *look for trends* in comments. Use comments to assist in understanding the "why" behind the data.

Often there can be isolated comments that are extremely negative and hurtful to individuals. Organizations and leaders need to avoid knee-jerk reactions to isolated comments. Seeking out the individual or in any way attempting to give any appearance of retaliation against someone who makes such comments will not lead to improving the employee experience, which is the objective for conducting a survey.

Unfortunately, we have seen too many leaders get stuck in the trap of focusing too heavily on isolated negative comments. If there is a trend of negative responses and the comments help in understanding a low score on a particular survey element, then they are useful.

If a vendor is not utilized, then the internal work of compiling, trending, and analyzing the data and comments is needed prior to the work sessions described above. This may mean that some of the more sophisticated statistical analysis that point to key factors of significance related to satisfaction or dissatisfaction may not be available. Additionally, benchmarking against other organizations will likely not be possible either. Yet, we see some organizations successfully surveying their employees using a tool such as Survey Monkey. Conducting a survey without a vendor is *always* preferable over not surveying employees due to financial constraints as long as a high-quality tool and a well-designed process are utilized.

Putting Results to Work to Improve the Employee Experience

It's worth repeating that surveying and communicating results alone will not gain you improvements in the employee experience. Communicating results is not the same as using them to create change. While we do need a timely communication process and open disclosure, we must couple this with activities of performance improvement.

To kick off the communication of results, Jane and I recommend an organization-wide communication event. Since our partner hospitals have a process for quarterly employee forums, or town hall meetings, it is at these sessions that the CEO can provide a brief overview of the organization-wide results. This report can identify and celebrate the top improvements and overview the priority focus areas from an organization-wide perspective.

The CEO can communicate to employees how the organization-wide improvement efforts will proceed with the guidance of leaders and the Employee Experience Team. Emphasis should also be placed on expectations regarding the communication of department-specific results and the activities of goal setting and action planning at that level.

In organizations without an existing forum for group employee meetings, or in addition to these forums, a well-devised written communication from the CEO can be utilized.

On the department or work-unit level, each frontline leader should be required to conduct a survey-focused staff meeting. These department-level meeting activities have several objectives: presenting department results in comparison to the organization's overall results and the results of other departments, presenting the trending of department results in comparison to prior years, recognizing and celebrating trends of improvement, identifying the top priorities for future improvement, and developing a goal and initial action plan for improvement. Setting a time frame in which all leaders conduct these meetings is helpful in creating accountability.

Sample Department Meeting Agenda

1. Review of organization's survey results (multi-year trends, if available)

2. Improvements since last survey

3. Identified opportunities to improve

4. Organization's goal for improving the employee experience (if one has been set)

5. Review of department's survey results (multi-year trends, if available)

6. Improvements since last survey

7. Identified opportunities to improve

8. Review of opportunities to improve

   a. Prioritize one to three top issues

   a. Develop department-specific goal

9. Identification of action steps, responsibilities, and follow-up process

10. Evaluation of the meeting

While conducting this department meeting, the leader should be non-defensive about the results and avoid asking confronting questions. Leaders should be careful to not dismiss suggestions or discount individual contributions. Statements by leaders which in any way give the perception of retaliation or punishment for rating the workplace or leadership poorly cannot be tolerated by the organization. If a leader has difficulty with facilitating such a meeting, it may be best to have this session facilitated by a senior leader or a high-performing employee in the department.

These should be well-facilitated sessions that create trust and openness regarding the survey process and results. Mutual respect and open dialogue are valuable as you strive to identify priorities and develop action plans. I always found that having a few visuals on a slide as well as a handout that overviewed the results were helpful. Using a flip chart to facilitate the discussion about priorities and action plans was also helpful as it increases the employees' perception of being heard. As with all good action plans, individuals should be assigned tasks, timelines should be set, and check-in processes should be adhered to.

An example of great leader facilitation sounds like this: "The survey results showed that we have very few 'strongly satisfied' responses related to performance feedback. The survey comments in this area trend toward a concern regarding the annual performance evaluation and day-to-day feedback. Do you have further information that can help to clarify this finding? What actions do you feel are important related to evaluations and feedback?" After such an opening statement, the leader or facilitator's role is to *listen*.

An opportunity for employees to evaluate a leader's facilitation of these meetings is a tactic that Jane and I highly recommend. The meeting evaluation can be a simple form that is completed by all attendees. The evaluations can be submitted to one designated employee who is responsible to deliver them to the applicable leader or team who is overseeing the survey rollout process. If this isn't part of your organization's overall process, you may still want to incorporate an evaluation so that you can continue to improve this process each year. The following example could be adopted by you or your entire organization.

Sample Department Survey Results and Planning Meeting Evaluation

Respond: Strongly Disagree, Disagree, Neutral, Agree, or Strongly Agree

Please add comments to help us understand your responses.

1. The organization's survey results were reported in a manner that was understandable.

2. The department's survey results were reported in a manner that was understandable.

3. The leader was able to facilitate a discussion that led to priority improvement areas being identified and agreed upon.

4. The leader was able to facilitate a discussion that led to initial action steps for improvement of one or more of the priority areas.

5. I am confident that this year's survey results and follow-up activities will lead to improvement in the identified priority areas.

6. Please provide any additional comments in regard to this meeting.

Frontline leaders can be held accountable for holding these meetings by senior leadership communicating a deadline and transparently reporting compliance with the deadline.

Frontline leaders can also be held accountable for improvements via a monthly meeting with their senior leaders during which they report on their improvement action plans and any interim data or feedback regarding how the plans are working. Reaching goals for improving the employee experience may be an element on the leader's annual performance evaluation.

In addition to the department-specific improvement efforts, we recommend that the Employee Experience Team, in keeping with any organization-wide goal that has been set, create an annual action plan. The action plan is broken down into quarterly action plans that guide their team's activities.

In organizations without a designated Employee Experience Team, we recommend the creation of twelve-week teams. These twelve-week teams are made up of ten or so of your organization's high-performing employees. They select one priority item identified on the survey and create an action plan that can be implemented in twelve weeks or less. Once this team has accomplished their aim, they disband and another twelve-week team is assembled. These teams are often led by a leader, yet employee populated and driven. Often leadership support is needed to assist in navigating the organization's procedures and accessing any necessary approvals and resources related to the team's action plans.

The Employee Experience Team or Twelve-Week Teams can be held accountable through the frequent reporting of their progress to a senior leadership team or sponsor.

Monitoring Improvement Efforts

Many organizations survey the employee experience on an annual basis. Then they set an organization-wide goal and department-specific goals for improvement. Some examples of organization-wide and department-specific goals are shown in Appendix 12.

When it comes to annual goals linked to annual survey results, you are going to want to get frequent feedback on whether or not your improvement plans are working. You will want to monitor to see if you are trending to meet your goal. To aid in that, some vendors offer a midyear or quarterly survey that is a smaller survey focused on the key elements that align to the organization and department goals.

In some instances, this may not be offered by your vendor, or it may be cost prohibitive. There are some low-cost ways to approach regular monitoring of your progress. To regularly monitor the status of overall satisfaction and the organization-wide goal, these elements could be surveyed as part of the evaluation of quarterly employee forums or town hall meetings. Or an internal survey could be developed and administered quarterly, or semi-annually, focusing again on the applicable subset of the survey elements.

At the department level, the status of employee satisfaction or engagement can be regularly monitored by a simple exercise at staff meetings. The leader can facilitate a session in which employees indicate whether the selected priority elements are improving, staying the same, or getting worse. A discussion surrounding employee perceptions of improvement (or not) can then lead to amendments in the action plan. In some departments, we have seen them enlist the help of their human resources department to conduct a mini email survey of the department. These results are then presented and discussed at a staff meeting.

Call to Action

The commitment to the measurement and improvement of the employee experience is a testament to the organization's culture and values surrounding peak performance.

These efforts can lead you to improved relationships; engaged, motivated, and loyal employees; reduced turnover and absenteeism; increased productivity; improved quality and service; and, in the end, achievement of organizational goals and peak results.

Take the time to assess your current practices surrounding surveying and improving the employee experience. Identify and act on opportunities to take these practices to greater levels to produce excellent results for your organization.

The following Success Plan can serve as a guide through this discovery and improvement process.

Surveying and Improving the Employee Experience Success Plan

Evaluate Current State

- Review currently utilized surveys on a department-specific or organization-wide level. How often are they administered? In-house or outside vendor? What is the process and time frame adopted for surveying, communicating, and using results? Is there a process for interim mini-surveys to check on the progress of action plans?

▪ Evaluate the trend of results in your organization and/ or department. If you are a frontline leader, how does your department compare to other departments and the organization? How does your department compare to benchmarks?

▪ What are the organization's and/or department's goals or priorities for improving the employee experience? What action plans are being developed to do so?

Plan and Make Improvements— Select and Prioritize Based on Assessment

If no survey process exists in your organization or department:

▪ Organize a team to develop or select a survey tool.

▪ Initiate the survey and implement plans for a high response rate.

▪ Analyze results.

▪ Communicate results to employees in a timely fashion.

▪ Facilitate the selection of an improvement priority or priorities (no more than three).

▪ Facilitate the development of an action plan.

If survey process is in place for your organization and/or department:

- Develop and implement plans for a higher response rate.

- Develop and implement plans for a timely communication and use of results for goal setting and action planning.

- **Organization Change Agent:** Advocate for an organization-wide survey that is consistently administered and is utilized for continual improvement to the employee experience.

Evaluate and Adjust

- Develop and implement a plan for the monitoring of the results of the improvement efforts through more frequent mini-surveys.

- Regularly reassess to evaluate if the changes are leading to improvements. Adjust plan and improvement activities as necessary. Refer to Solution Twelve for additional guidance.

Resiliency

Resiliency:

1. The ability of an object to spring back into shape; elasticity.

2. The capacity to recover quickly from difficulties; toughness.

3. The capacity to withstand stress.

Y ou may be wondering what the topic of resiliency is doing in a book on leading your employees to peak performance. Fair question. As Sue and I have traveled across the country working closely with leaders in organizations big and small, we've observed that the pressures and stressors of being a leader are greater than ever.

The turnover in leadership positions is often very high. And leaders often admit to us that their personal resiliency is very low. Sue and I were leaders for a combined forty-five years and, therefore, have personal experience with the stressors of leadership—both from senior leadership (leading leaders) and frontline leadership (leading employees) perspectives.

One thing that leaders, and not just those in healthcare, realize is that the resources of time and money to be able to effectively do our jobs are not likely going to increase. I have never worked with a CEO who said to me, "Jane, you are looking a little frazzled. It's budget time. How about you budget for as many new positions as you need to assist you and I will make it happen?"

I valued the CEOs I worked with, and they valued me. Yet, this didn't make unlimited resources available to me. Most often, the message sounded more like: "We need to do more with less." The stressors in the lives of leaders are not going away. This necessitates the creation of a plan to effectively deal with stress. All leaders and employees can benefit from making a resiliency plan and sticking to it.

Sue and I have learned that it takes healthy, resilient leaders and employees to achieve great results. We also know that it's not all about work. Your personal life needs attention just like the strategy and goals of your organization. When you put effort into nurturing both, you can become unstoppable!

Sue and I are truly concerned about leaders and the stresses they face. When leaders fail, companies can fail. That is why our company includes a training module on stress, work-life balance, and resiliency at all of our public training offerings for leaders. We continue this same commitment through our writing.

Bryan Sexton from the Duke Patient Safety Center stated in a lecture that I attended, "Those with tenacity, dedication, and a strong sense of responsibility are subject to burnout." Who do you know with more tenacity, dedication, and sense of responsibility than a leader? Maybe a Navy Seal?

Dr. Sexton also promotes the view that burnout is a work problem and not a personality problem. I could not agree more. I spent a large part of my early leadership career listening to leaders around me who were complaining they were "burnt out." I would think, *what a wimp. Put your big-girl panties on and deal with it.* The unfortunate part is that leaders leave their jobs when they feel this burnout.

Yet all of us experience times in our lives when our resiliency is at an all-time low. There may be tragedy in our lives or a severe loss we are attempting to recover from. When we do not recover from each event, soon even the small things become big things.

Building resiliency allows leaders and employees the ability to "bounce back" in response to life and work stressors.

There was a time in my life when my resiliency was at an all-time low. I was serving as the vice president of nursing of a community hospital. It was a position I had hoped for and prepared for my entire career, and I looked forward to every moment. I truly felt that my leadership was going to make a difference for the leaders, patients, physicians, and nurses that I served.

I thought I would be in this role until retirement. It didn't work out that way. I spent five years in this position and moved on to another.

My memories of holding this position are mostly bad ones. The negativity was screaming at me, and positivity was only whispering. In reflection, I know that I made a difference while in the position, and others have told me that I did. However, what went terribly wrong was my lack of self-care. I was not taking care of myself or caring for my personal life so that I could function at the higher level of stress I had moved into when assuming this position.

I had experienced a tragedy in my personal life, and instead of taking into account that this may need to be taken care of, I just plowed on and worked more. I put my personal troubles in a box with a pretty ribbon on a shelf in my mind and determined I would deal with it "when I had time."

I worked so many hours that I neglected important personal relationships around me. I gave up exercise, sleeping, and eating well. My weight and stress level skyrocketed, and my energy plummeted.

One snowy February, I was getting out of my car to trudge to my office. Like most days, I was coming to work in the dark and leaving in the dark. I stopped in the middle of the street, in shock at a realization that hit me. I had forgotten my mother's birthday! I don't mean by a day—I forgot it by a week! My mother, who celebrates *everything*, was likely still waiting by the phone for my call. It was a wakeup call that I was on a very bad road.

Not long after, another leadership position opened in my organization, and I took it. When Sue and I met at a coffee shop for me to break the news to her, she asked me why I was leaving. She knew I had been preparing for the senior leader level of leadership for nearly a decade and that it had been my dream.

My explanation to her was, "Something feels very bad. I know that I need to step back and take care of myself and my family. I don't know what it is, but I can feel it."

Since that time, my knowledge and my habits of self-care have improved my resiliency. I am confident that I would deal with the stressors of high-level leadership much differently today.

I realize in looking back at those years that the issue was that my resiliency was at zero. It is difficult when you are in the middle of chaos to see outside of the whirlwind you are living in each and every day. Instead of looking in the mirror, I blamed the job and ran from it when I first had the chance.

A plan to increase your resiliency, and keep it at a high level, is vital to staying in the jobs you love. Leaders are so essential to every great company and every employee experience, and the care of leaders is essential too.

Resiliency assists you in every aspect of your life, no matter what is hurled at you. In a phrase, we can all learn to duck and pop back up.

Creating a Plan for Resiliency

There are several things that can contribute to improving your personal resiliency. The following key items that contribute to self-care and resiliency may be things you have never considered before. Take time to reflect on each, and determine which of them may be focuses of further action. Our hope is that if you don't have a plan for your resiliency or your plan isn't working, you create a personal resiliency plan, while recognizing that this isn't a selfish act.

Sue and I always advocate that every plan include two or three clear action steps that you can commit razor-sharp focus to. The important part is to just start. You will find that you feel better and in more control of your life and circumstances by having a plan and committing to a small number of changes.

Maintain close relationships with family and friends. I mentioned earlier that when I was at my lowest point of resiliency, I had to leave my dream job. During that time, I let go of the things that could have helped me through the turmoil. I let go of important relationships I had built over my lifetime.

All of us can probably think of those friends we have that can go without even a phone call for months at a time, but when you do call them, you strike right back up where you left off. Those friends are few and far between. Most relationships take care and nurturing.

I think about a leader's life as a juggling act. The difference between you and the typical juggler on a street corner in New York City is that your balls are not made of rubber and don't bounce back. They are made of glass. And close relationships with family and friends are glass balls. Dropping one is not an option.

Make your relationships one of your "big rocks." The big rocks in your day, week, month, and year are those things that you put at a higher priority than anything else in your life. If you were filling a bucket and were told that you had to fit so many rocks in the bucket, you would put the big ones in first, right? Then, all the little rocks get filled in around them. When your relationships are your big rocks, they get attention in your resiliency plan daily or weekly.

Cherishing and nurturing relationships is not work, it is fun. Date your significant other. Read to your children or grandchildren. Play outside with them. Call a friend or meet for coffee, giving him or her your full attention. Call your parents or adult children every Sunday, creating a tradition they can count on and will look forward to each week. Go for a walk with a co-worker. Send birthday cards with a personal note. You get the idea. Quality time.

Have a positive view of yourself and confidence in your abilities and strengths. Knowing what you are good at is imperative to resiliency. Make a list of what's great about ME. If you are constantly walking around saying, "I cannot handle this. I cannot stand it anymore," you will not be able to overcome the events that are draining your resiliency away.

I spent a lot of time in my vice president position blaming others for their bad behavior and its effect on me. If THEY would just do their jobs, or if THEY would just feel the same way I did and would agree with MY view, then all would be right with the world, and I would be able to manage much easier. At times of low resiliency, I was constantly blaming others! If I had thought of myself as resilient, instead of right, I would have sought a way to frame their behaviors positively. Maybe I would have stopped to listen to their viewpoint and to consider that it may be an easy compromise or at least a way to agree to disagree.

As a leader you must take time to reflect on where you have opportunities to grow and develop, but this shouldn't be at the expense of limiting the celebration of your strengths. And a healthy way of focusing on what you may not be the best at is to consider the strengths of others. For instance, you may recognize that a member of your team is more creative than you. Wonderful! This can be your go-to person when the department's communication board needs decorating and updating. Delegate the task instead of beating yourself up about how bad the board looks! Focus on what you do really well, and be proud and happy of your strengths and results.

Work on your ability to manage strong feelings and impulses. By strong feelings and impulses, I mean primarily anger. As leaders, we often do not get an opportunity to have a reaction to an event twice. Especially when a crisis hits, we are on stage and the spotlights on us are shining brightly. Our behaviors and reactions are noticed and scrutinized. There may be times in your life that you wish you could take words back or redo your reactions to situations. Preventing future mistakes of this nature takes practice to respond professionally when emotions like anger and frustration are high in a public, and even private, interaction.

Managing strong feelings and impulses requires you to draw on diplomacy, inner strength, and positivity. Contrast this with the sudden flash of anger that allows toxic negativity to swarm your brain and keep you from thinking and reacting reasonably. In some situations, the right response may be to step away from the problem and go somewhere to think and reason. Then when you have investigated, contemplated, and reasoned, you will find the healthiest way to solve a problem. I love the "Keep Calm and Carry On" saying. It fits here.

Cope with stress in healthy ways. Avoid unhealthy coping mechanisms such as reliance on substances (e.g., drugs, alcohol, food, etc.). I cannot begin to count the number of times I overindulged on chocolate or sweets with the thought running through my weakened brain, "I have had a stressful day. I deserve a treat."

How many times do we hear in the workplace, "This is going to be a wine night?" I have agreed with that statement many times. Having a glass of wine (in moderation!) with friends and venting about a situation that is stressful is actually healthy. In fact, it usually results in another healthy coping mechanism: laughter!

You may need to assess how you may be relying on an indulgence, compulsion, or any other unhealthy coping mechanisms. You may need to have this conversation with your spouse or a close friend to see if they recognize unhealthy coping mechanisms or responses to stress.

Next, move on to find healthy ways to counter stress. It may be exercise, which can be as simple as taking a walk. It really works. So does deep breathing and meditation, even for two minutes. Or it might be listening to music or watching a funny movie or sitcom. I'm a big fan of *The Big Bang Theory* as a stress reliever.

Focus on finding your ticket out of stress. Find something healthy that feeds you and calms you, and make this part of your resiliency plan. Only then will the unhealthy donut binge happen way less often.

Sue and I have worked together for more than two decades. Over these many years, I've observed that it's not her nature to be a "stress eater." This is one way in which we differ, and I've always marveled at her restraint during times of stress.

So it was quite surprising when I realized that she had suddenly slipped into eating as a response to a period of high stress. One summer, many years ago, Sue was heading up the project team that was opening a new inpatient psychiatric service line. It was an unusual project timeline. The project got its start on July 5 of that year and needed to be totally operational by October 1, as the opening had to coincide with the start of the hospital's fiscal year. If this target opening date was not met, all of the effort would have to be shelved until October 1 of the following year.

This project required a major renovation to an old Air Force base hospital. It required recruitment of psychiatrists and employees. The federal and state regulatory requirements were arduous. The task list was huge. Each day, there was an understanding that if that day's action steps weren't accomplished, there was a high likelihood that the October 1 deadline would not be met.

This story had a happy ending as the new service was opened that year as planned.

When discussing this project (which she refers to as Project Slamming), Sue often mentions that she doesn't recall much else that happened in the world or in her life that entire summer. And she also admits, as I observed, that she took on the habit of stress eating during this project.

Down the hallway from the administrative offices, there was a kitchenette. Unfortunately, during that time, we kept it stocked with comfort food. By that I mean unhealthy food. Sue's work hours extended from early in the morning to late at night, weekends included, during this project. And if there were surveillance cameras in that hallway, you could have watched her making frequent trips from her office to that kitchenette at all hours of the day and night. In fact, had the carpet in that hallway been lined with corn chips and cookies, you would have discovered her path each morning from the night before!

Fortunately, when the project was completed and the stress level reduced, it became apparent that Sue's unhealthy habit of stress eating was just temporary and situational. Thankfully she hadn't engaged in other unhealthy coping habits that may have been harder to cease, such as alcohol or drugs.

Help others. I have a friend who, by far, is the most altruistic person I know. Her name is Jan. Jan does not have a lot of money to give away and therefore does not give those types of gifts. More impressively, she gives of herself, in the service of others, often. She is truly an example of the altruistic human and is a person I consider to be very resilient, despite great stressors in her life.

The very act of focusing on the needs of others and giving of yourself to others causes your brain to react in the same way as it does to seeing positivity. These actions lead to a flood of the love hormone oxytocin. Liken it to a zero-calorie dose of chocolate for you. Jan is a walking love hormone. I personally feel that doing good things for others who are in need makes you grateful and positive about your own state of affairs. Definitely another tool to build your resilience!

See positive in your life, in spite of the stressors. The information on recognition, celebration, and appreciation in Solution Three stresses the importance of positivity and its effect on your brain and leadership style. Framing things positively can also help with your resiliency. If you cannot see anything positive about a situation, remember what your brain will do. When you only see the negative, you will not light up the "3 Cs" —Communication, Collaboration, and Critical thinking. When your brain closes down on a problem and only sees the negative, you likely won't be able to resolve your crisis effectively.

This takes training and effort to look at the glass half full, or full, in every situation. This may take a few hours or an ability to "sleep on it," but when you get to the point of viewing something positively, you will be more able to see your way out of the situation. Practice positivity by writing down three good things that happen to you daily. A practice of this nature is explained in more detail in Solution Three.

Creating your island of inaccessibility. Ah, create a deserted island just for yourself. Go to it every day, no matter what. This is what you do for yourself to recharge. This is not a luxury. This is a necessity.

I'll share a story about Kim, who has been the leader in an outpatient surgery center in California for thirty-two years. When Kim attended one of our training Summits, she asked if she could describe to me her island of inaccessibility so she could "make sure she was doing it right." She went on to describe the lunch routine each day at work. As the leader, she attempts to make sure that the employees get their much-needed lunch breaks so that they can nourish themselves and rest. She eats lunch last.

Then, after eating her lunch in a very brisk fashion, she sets down her pager and cell phone on her desk. She then walks out of the building without telling anyone she is leaving or where she is going.

She proceeds to walk in the neighborhoods surrounding the hospital. She attempts to clear her mind of the stress that she has going on at work. Whenever her brain strays from the beauty around her to a work problem, she stops walking. She then looks for a plant, an animal, or a child. She feels that those three things connect her to enjoying life without all of the adult worries. When she is able to forget for even one moment or two about the stressors she has back inside the walls of her hospital, she walks again. Some days she makes it around the block, some days she does not.

After just twenty minutes away, she goes back to work

and straps back on the technology that keeps her connected to the stress. She climbs back into the work she left briefly.

She also reported that not one employee has ever said, "Where were you? We needed you!" And she has been able to manage in that high-stress position for thirty-two years.

Yes, Kim. I believe you are "doing it right."

Create your island. And create your plan for getting there. Determine three or four things that really, truly feed you and engage in one for thirty to ninety minutes every single day. Is it reading a book for fun with your feet up? Is it taking a bubble bath? Getting a massage? Drinking coffee in front of a fireplace every morning? Watching a funny movie? Or taking a walk like Kim?

Take a technology break. Your island of inaccessibility may qualify as a technology break, but often we need more of this. Our work and personal lives are overlapping today in a very negative way. Leaders have a difficult time "unplugging or disconnecting" from work. The reason may be that the very device you use to stay connected to work is the same one you use to stay connected to your friends and family. Take a stance right away on your use of technology. Can you go a day without checking your Facebook page? Can you go a day without checking your work emails? Whether or not you feel burnout from technology now, take a proactive stance toward preventing it.

Sleep well. Our sleep is important. It heals our brains and gives us emotional regulation that puts things in perspective. I read an article recently where a physician wrote, "Sleep is no longer thought of as putting your car in the garage, shutting off the light, and just parking it there to do nothing all night long." Sleep is important for us to heal and face another day. It is to be treasured and cared for. If you are not a good sleeper, seek help!

Eat well. Your body is a machine that needs fuel to power its energy, enthusiasm, and efficiency. Over the course of a thirty-two-year career in nursing, I have seen people suffer from chronic diseases that are completely preventable and mainly caused by our diet in America. It is affecting us at a younger and younger age. The American food system is making us ill and obese. Feed yourself well and with foods that are real, not processed.

Notice how I am not advocating that you go on a "diet," or to eat a combination of certain foods? How you feed yourself emotionally, physically, and spiritually is such a personal thing. Find out what your version of personal health is and when you feel good. Eat more of the things that make you feel healthy and less of the things that don't. It can be that simple of a plan.

Move well. Move every day, for just ten minutes at a time if you cannot find a span of time longer than that. Choose a form of exercise that makes you happy and is fun to do, and just do it! Changing up your exercise routine from time to time can be helpful too. There are so many great articles and books written on the mental, emotional, and, of course, physical benefits of exercise. Exercise is just as important as sleep is for healing and energizing you.

Be an Inspiration

When you adopt a practice of resiliency, you lead by example. Not only will you be healthier, you may be a role model and an inspiration to others! You may be thinking to yourself that you certainly do not want to become a life coach to your employees.

When you think back on one-on-one employee conversations over the course of your leadership career, how many of them were initiated because one of your employees was exhibiting behaviors that were affecting the rest of your team? How many of your employees have confided to you in a statement much like this one: "I am having a lot of stress at home. I know I am showing it at work."

You are likely already discussing resiliency and coping mechanisms with your team. What if you had a practice that was successful for you that you could share with them?

Even if you are not comfortable having conversations on this topic with your employees, they will likely notice that you have changed something about yourself. They will notice when you advocate for yourself by taking an exercise class after work and leaving in a timely manner to get there. They may notice that you take the opportunity to get outside to turn your face to the sun for ten minutes at lunchtime.

It is an extraordinary leader who advocates for his or her personal health and encourages others to do so as well.

Be an Organizational Change Agent

Sue and I were very fortunate to work together for an employer that recognized that health and wellness were important long before other employers caught on. The research findings have become more plentiful in regard to the link between healthy employees and their performance and productivity.

We truly believe that creating an amazing employee experience means creating a work culture where self-care is not a luxury but a priority. It is an expectation that your employees will care for themselves, and an employer can help.

You read in Solution Five that work-life balance is often very important for your employees that are millennials and Gen Xers. They are the up-and-coming majority in the workforce. Therefore, wellness and work-life balance strategies take on a new level of importance in creating an optimal employee experience.

Sue wrote in Solution Four that we should look for certain qualities when hiring. Isn't self-care a behavior you should look for in a future employee? Won't those people with a plan for their own personal resiliency be a step ahead of others? Your hiring and retention strategies should take resiliency into consideration.

Improving resiliency can be a key action in your organization's plan to achieve peak performance. If your organization doesn't already have a dedicated department or team that is responsible for making this happen, consider asking an Employee Experience Team to take this on. And if you have an employee-driven Training Team, they can be helpful in these efforts as well. These are strategic actions that can add value *and* create fun at work.

Call to Action

My "running away" from a job that I loved was essentially escaping the bad things that were happening to me every day at work. Happy, resilient people still have just as many bad things happen to them as the rest of us. They simply reflect upon them, deal with them, and move on. I didn't do that. I was instead dwelling on the negativity at work each day, until I could no longer see happiness there.

We love Barbara Frederickson's work on positivity. Her formula is simple. Happy people experience more happy emotions than negative emotions. The negative emotions may be just as intense but are overshadowed by the person's ability to see happiness, instead of dwelling on the negativity.

What if the cause of your stress is chronic and appears never ending? And you've tried new tactics, and things still seem hopeless? In this situation, professional help is likely needed. Recognizing and acting on this need may be difficult. I have relied on professional counseling several times in my adulthood. During those times that I did seek this level of help, I was indeed in crisis. I wish I had gone more readily and earlier. It was always so helpful to talk to a professional and have the assurance that my response and feelings were all pretty normal. It helps to see that you are not the only negativity dweller and stress carrier in the world!

Your ability to be resilient, to see a place for yourself in a job and life that makes you happy, takes work on your part. And this may be the most important work you'll ever do.

At all of the public training events that our company has held since its inception, we donate a portion of the registration fees to a local non-profit charity organization that is doing great things to serve others in the community in which our events are held. At one recent event, when the organization's representative attended our event to accept the donation, she addressed our audience with this great message:

Self-care is critical to having a strong inner foundation.
Taking care of you means that the people in your life will
receive the best of you, rather than what is left of you.
—Lorraine Cohen

Resiliency Success Plan

Evaluate Current State

- Take a resiliency test or quiz as a current baseline starting point. There are many available on the Internet (e.g., "the Resilience Scale, etc.).

- Engage in some reflection. Assess how you feel. Do you feel burned out? Do you feel as though you are in a situation with no way out? Assess how others have been treating you. Have the people around you been worried about you? Assess your emotional health. Are you happy?

- Assess your physical health. Do you have physical symptoms that may be caused by stress?

- Reflect on the current actions you take to decrease stress and improve your health and resiliency. Are you doing enough, or the right things, given your assessment findings above?

- Review the organization's and/or your department's priorities and strategies for decreasing burnout, increasing resiliency, and improving wellness.

Plan and Make Improvements—
Select and Prioritize Based on Assessment

- Create (or revise) your plan for resiliency. Put your plan in writing. As you were reading about the tactics to improve resiliency, did you note any that struck you as really missing from your life? Start there to create a plan for your personal resiliency. If you don't know where to start, I often recommend the island of inaccessibility and taking a technology break. Don't make too many changes at once. Choose one new resiliency tactic and commit to it as a thirty-day challenge. Then challenge yourself to add a new resiliency tactic every thirty days until you have a complement of tactics that work for you.

- Tell others who are close to you about your plan for resiliency. Support during change is always helpful. This can also serve as an accountability tactic. By having people around you be your accountability partners, you will be encouraging them as well.

- **Organization Change Agent:** Advocate for an organization-wide strategy and action plan focused on decreasing burnout, increasing resiliency, and improving wellness.

- **Organizational Change Agent:** Role model healthy resiliency behaviors to inspire others. Initiate efforts on a smaller scale within your span of control, such as a healthy lunch club or an organized walk each day.

- **Organizational Change Agent:** If there is a team such as the Employee Experience Team or an Employee Training Team, appeal to them to assist in these efforts.

Evaluate and Adjust Plan

- Evaluate how you feel often. Keep a journal. Or better yet, keep two journals. My friend James recommends that you have two journals, one for "good days" and one specifically for "bad days." In your good day journal, you write all of the good things that happen to you each day. We advocate you write down at least three good things. This journal should have a cool saying on the outside of it, and it should be your favorite color. You should love this journal. Then, when those bad days happen, write in the bad day journal. This one should be plain and have a black cover. Your writing in this journal helps you to process your thoughts and emotions related to the bad day. Then we challenge you to write down three good things in your good day journal even on a bad day. These journals are tools that you can use to look back and reflect on your resiliency.

- Regularly reassess. Are the activities of your resiliency plan leading to improvements? Look back at certain intervals (quarterly, biannually, and annually) at the assessment activities listed above in the Current State Assessment. Repeat the resiliency test and compare it to your baseline. Reflect regarding how you feel. Reassess your physical health. Are things getting better? Or worse? What does this mean for changes to your resiliency plan?

■ Regularly reassess the organization's efforts and the results being achieved. How does the plan need to be changed based on the reassessment findings? See Solution Twelve for guidance.

Review, Readjust, Refresh, Reconnect, and Re-Inspire

John P. Kotter, Emeritus at the Harvard Business School and guru on leadership, reports that 70 percent of transformational change efforts fail. Leadership is hard. Change is hard. This book is filled with suggestions for change, and we want you to succeed with each one you initiate.

Over a career, leaders are going to take on many projects and a variety of improvement initiatives. This solution can provide tactics that move leaders beyond all of the "planning and doing" and on to the "evaluating and adjusting" that is recommended to achieve peak performance.

A best practice in creating successful change requires us to circle back to initiatives that have been planned and implemented. The initial assessing, planning, and implementation activities (i.e., Plan-Do) will get *good* results, while the follow-up activities of evaluating and adjusting (i.e., Study-Adjust) will lead to *great* results. These steps (Plan-Do-Study-Adjust) are repeated over and over as part of a cycle of continual improvement.

If the improvement cycle is shortchanged, the results will be shortchanged. A lack of evaluating and adjusting can also lead to an endless trail of "start-stop-start-stop" activities as planned changes are initiated, and then stopped, in a flavor-of-the-month fashion. This type of dysfunction can create confusion, diminish trust, and waste valuable and limited resources.

To succeed in this regard, Jane and I recommend that the focus of evaluation and adjustment include opportunities to review, readjust, refresh, reconnect, and re-inspire.

Review

When it comes to conducting a review, look for the observable impacts of the planned change. The review activities can include self-reflection, assessment, analysis of applicable data, and focused rounding discussions with key stakeholders that were impacted.

Key Review Questions

1. Did the change result in an improvement?

2. Was the improvement to the level desired (e.g., was the goal met)?

3. Is the impact of the change measurable? If so, what are the measurable changes?

4. Was the change worth the investment of time and resources?

5. Were there any unintended effects from the change? Were there any surprises?

6. Is the change standardized? Is there a new standardized process that has been adopted by all? If not, what got in the way of standardization and adoption?

7. What lessons were learned?

8. What knowledge was gained?

9. If you had to do it all over again, what would you do?

You will want to reflect on the details of your original action plan to evaluate for elements of the change that were not implemented. Maybe these elements were intentionally tabled for a later phase of change. Or, maybe you decided to modify the recommended tactic in some fashion. If so, now it is time to evaluate the impact and determine if another phase of change is needed to get the desired great results.

As you move through this review process, you will identify signs of progress and success, as well as any problems or areas for further improvement. You will want to take time to celebrate your progress and the lessons learned as you move forward to plan and execute further improvements toward standardizing the new practices.

Moving beyond the activities of planning and implementation and into the review phase proved to be life-saving in a hospital quality-improvement project I was involved in. I was part of a multidisciplinary team of leaders and clinicians that was charged to decrease deaths of patients with a specific disease process. When concluding the plan-do steps of this project, I recall that familiar tug to move on to the next process that needed improving. Yet, being true to the Plan-Do-Study-Adjust cycle, the team engaged in a thorough review as part of the study phase. The team learned that, indeed, the changes had led to some improvements. Yet the team's efforts had not achieved the expected level of improvement that they had set as their aim.

The team approached this review finding with intent to learn why. And the answers they discovered in this review led to additional planning and action steps to be executed in the adjust phase. As a result of being diligent and taking the time and energy to review and adjust, the reduction in deaths exceeded the team's initial goal. I recall one of the team's physicians stating at one of the review sessions, "We may not be at the patients' bedsides, yet we are saving lives through our work around this table here today."

Readjust

Often after the review activities are complete, the adjustments that are needed become clear. As in the example above, optimal results would have been forgone if the team had swiftly moved on to the next thing that needed to be improved.

A new leader that I had mentored quickly adopted employee rounding as a priority leadership tactic. She was committed to developing relationships with her employees and believed in the benefits of employee rounding. A year in to her leadership role, while reviewing her employee satisfaction data, she realized there was improvement in her overall employee satisfaction results, with the exception of those who worked the midnight shift.

With this review finding, this leader reflected on her rounding efforts. She came to realize that she had not developed a systematic process for rounding on her employees who worked the midnight shifts. She was gaining benefits from employee rounding, yet not to the full extent she could. In the readjustment phase, she created a plan for conducting employee rounding on the midnight shift.

With any adjustment opportunities you identify, you will want to create an action plan to make these additional modifications happen. A plan for adjustment includes many of the same elements as an initial project plan, such as identifying the action steps to be completed, the time frame, and the resources of time, talent, and money needed. Then, just start!

Once you have made these readjustments, you will want to circle back and review again. The leader who adjusted her plan to round on her midnight shift would certainly want to review the employee satisfaction results to check in on the results of her efforts.

Refresh

Congratulations if your review confirmed that you have made changes that are getting you, your team, and your organization the improved results that you targeted. If you didn't identify any additional adjustments you need to make to your implementation plan, you may now want to think about how to keep this tactic exciting, fresh, and alive. Leaders we coach often tell us that they, and their employees, want to avoid the mundane when standardizing great tactics.

So what does keeping an initiative fresh look like? For employee rounding, it may mean changing up a question or two. For behavior-based interviewing, it may mean training a new team member or two to join the panel interview team. For on-boarding, it may mean changing up the day-one welcome events. For thank-you notes to home, you may now want to extend your appreciation to family members of your employees.

While there are traditions that are good to hold onto, sometimes they can lose their appeal, excitement, and energy for those who have been engaged in them year after year.

Ask leaders. Ask your employees. They can provide feedback on initiatives that are no longer creating positive energy in your work environment. If these initiatives are important to peak performance in your organization, target them for "refreshment."

Reconnect

As an organization builds an arsenal of high-performance work practices such as the solutions included in this book, these existing practices can be connected to future initiatives. An organization doesn't have to always keep layering on new practices when the existing ones are known and are achieving great results.

A good time to consider connecting existing practices to

new initiatives may be when major strategic priorities or goals are adopted. Leaders can approach these new priorities and goals with the existing best practices or tactics in mind. Connect the dots between the existing tactic and how it can help in your new efforts. As your leadership, your work unit, and your organization evolve, so can your application of these tactics.

As an example on a department level, the leader of a hospital housekeeping department reconnected their long-standing behavior-based interview process to their new goal to decrease absenteeism. Their interview questions needed to be updated to reflect this goal.

On an organization level, a hospital with well-defined behavior standards for many years realized that they needed to connect those standards to their new priority strategy of becoming a high-reliability organization. They realized that empowerment was a key tactic toward achieving high reliability, yet the current behavior standards did not reflect an emphasis on empowerment. The Employee Experience Team was charged with reconnecting the standards to this new strategic priority.

Each time you are faced with a new strategic priority or goal, you may not need to look for new tactics for your action plan. You likely can utilize existing tactics with new focus and emphasis.

Re-Inspire

When you are achieving results, celebration can help to inspire the standardization of the change. We often need to be very deliberate in crediting our current success to the tactics that are working to create it. This can be a needed inspiration to continue with a change.

Some leaders find it inspiring to share a best practice that they have successfully adopted. Maybe they mentor other leaders or maybe they champion the change for their entire organization.

You may often engage in celebration and sharing in the early months and years of a successful change, yet many successful changes will need re-inspiration on a long-term and consistent basis.

When the reason for making the change is long forgotten, there is risk of reverting back to the old suboptimal way. This can happen even many years into an otherwise successful change effort.

As a leader who had a long tenure in an organization, I often served in the unofficial role as the "organization's historian." Having lived out two decades of an organization's history, I was able to contrast the past with the present. In our organization, that was the contrast of a problematic past to the current state of vast improvement. Often the past struggles and problems are forgotten as new people join the organization at a better point in its history. If tactics have been implemented that garner great results, many may not have known the organization prior to those tactics or results.

To re-inspire an organization to continue to utilize a tactic that is gaining long-term results, there may need to be a method of sharing the history of why the tactic was needed and how the tactic has achieved desired results.

Prior to adopting behavioral-based peer interviewing, one organization had a 27 percent employee turnover rate with the majority of turnover being in the first year. The change resulted in a decrease to 9 percent turnover. When a new leader joined the organization with its much-improved turnover rate, the new leader did not make the connection that the low turnover was linked to behavior-based peer interviewing. The new leader didn't experience the history that included the sense of urgency to fix the problem and the realization that behavior-based peer interviewing was the key tactic that got those improved results. Given this lack of understanding, the new leader did not keep a priority focus on behavior-based peer interviewing, which resulted in an increased turnover rate in her department.

Great tactics can fall by the wayside due to this lack of historical understanding. So, we need to be re-inspired by the "why" behind the current tactics that are utilized in our organizations to get great results. As a leader, you may need to seek out the "why," or you may need to paint the picture of the "why" to your employees.

For important initiatives to be kept alive, consider the tactic of creating "why boards." This board is a place for the team to display historical information on key tactics that were used to get great results. It is a way to re-inspire employees to keep on the path of continued efforts toward standardizing these tactics. A reminder that the tactic is not optional, that the tactic was the key to results and it shouldn't be lost. Each month, a different tactic could be highlighted on this board.

While the need to continually re-inspire might seem a bit frustrating to leaders, Jane and I encourage leaders to not skimp on opportunities to re-inspire your team by connecting them to the "why."

Call to Action

Change is not an event; it is a cycle. It is a cycle that leads to continual improvement. While leaders can focus a great majority of their efforts on assessing, planning, and implementing, Jane and I encourage you to continue through to the phases of evaluation and adjustment by engaging in activities to review, readjust, refresh, reconnect, and re-inspire. Taking these steps may be seen as extra work. No doubt, amending the way you approach change is hard work. However, it is required work to achieve peak performance!

The Framework for Achieving Great Results

The Capstone Team Structure

TEAM STRUCTURE

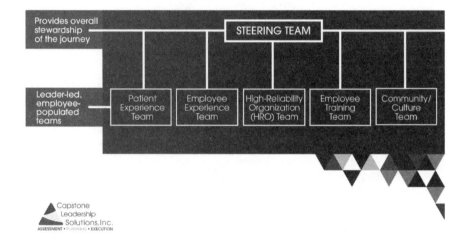

Capstone
Leadership
Solutions, Inc.
ASSESSMENT • PLANNING • EXECUTION

Department/Unit: _____

	Date	Employee Rounding Recommendation	Update
Accomplished			

	Date	Employee Rounding Recommendation	Update
In Progress			

	Date	Employee Rounding Recommendation	Why was it Tabled?
Tabled			

Note: Often this report is displayed in a colored format of green (Accomplished), yellow (In Progress), and red (Tabled); hence the name Stoplight Report.

Sample Hiring Decision Matrix

Candidate: _____ **Date:** ___/___/___

Education   1   2   3   4   5   × ____Weight = _____
Experience   1   2   3   4   5   × ____Weight = _____
Communication   1   2   3   4   5   × ____Weight = _____
Perceived "Fit"   1   2   3   4   5   × ____Weight = _____

Behavioral-based Interview Questions:
Question 1   1   2   3   4   5   × ____Weight = _____
Question 2   1   2   3   4   5   × ____Weight = _____
Question 3   1   2   3   4   5   × ____Weight = _____
Question 4   1   2   3   4   5   × ____Weight = _____
Question 5   1   2   3   4   5   × ____Weight = _____

TOTAL SCORE: _____

Recommend for Position: Yes   No

Comments:

Panel Member: _____

*Notes:

Weights must add up to 100 percent

Scoring is on a 1–5 scale with a 5 being the highest, most favorable response

Sample First Days' Checklist

Employee Name: _____ **Dept.:**_____

First Day of Work:_____

Date Submitted to Human Resources: _____

The First Days' Checklist	*Date Completed*	*Employee's Initials*	*Trainer's Initials*
Day 1			
Infectious Disease and Exposure Control Module/Test			
Hazardous Materials Awareness Module/Test and Access to MSDS			
Personal Protective Equipment (PPE) Module/Test			
Emergency Management Program Module/Test			
Abuse and Neglect Module/Test			
Fire and Safety Training Module/Test			
Review HR Module/Test (zero tolerance of alcohol and drugs, zero tolerance for harassment, employee's responsibility to maintain licensure/certificate, employee occurrence reporting, patient and resident rights)			

Review Work Rules and Regulations, Behavior Standards, Code of Ethics, Values			
Review Infection Control Policies			
Review HIPAA Policy			
Proper Lifting Techniques and Transfers (as well as other departmental safety requirements)			
Days 2–5			
Review Department-Specific Policy/Procedure Manual (process for scheduling time off work, calling in sick, scheduled breaks)			
Review Communication Standards/Plan Module/Test			
Review Administrative Policy/ Procedure Manual			
Review Occupational Health Policies (explain employee responsibility to complete OHS paperwork and medical testing if not completed at time of hire, annual TB testing, reporting of injuries, etc.)			
Review Chain of Command and Communication Policy			

Review Payroll Policy (Train on time clock, work schedules/shift rotation/shift differentials/overtime policy)			
Review Job Status/Explain FTE Status			
Review Orientation Period ("at-will" first 90 days; 30-day and 90-day check-ins; and 90-day evaluation; mid-year conversations, anniversary annual evaluation process)			
Review Basic Rules (dress code, smoke-free campus, parking)			

Sample Employee Experience Team Charter

Purpose

This team will strive to achieve employee engagement scores above the 95th percentile and help make our organization the employer of choice.

Ground Rules

- Give high priority to team meetings

- Be open-minded, respect viewpoints, take nothing personally

- Schedule all meetings in advance to minimize conflicts

- Involve all team members

- Abide by and support team decisions

- Collect sufficient data to support decisions

Tasks

- Plan, promote, and assist in Employee Activities

- Promote employee suggestions for the Suggestion Program

- Plan and promote communication of information to employees, including quarterly CEO town hall meetings

- Conduct exit and stay interviews

- Promote employee-to-employee recognition program

- Create annual goal and quarterly action plans based on Employee Engagement Survey and other assessment findings

Boundaries

- Plan activities within designated budget

- The Team has the authority to monitor employee engagement and report findings

- Make recommendations to the Steering Team, when applicable; recommendations must pertain to groups or entire workforce, not individuals

- The Team does not have the authority to make changes in personnel or initiate any type of corrective action

Meetings

- Meet biweekly with action assignments to be completed between meetings

- Meet as needed for special events and additionally as needed to accomplish our purpose

Measures of Success

- Quarterly Mini Satisfaction Surveys

- Annual Employee Engagement Survey

- Turnover Rate

Sample Behavior Standards Recommitment Form

Commitment to My Coworkers

- I will respect my fellow coworkers by not indulging in hurtful conversation (i.e., avoid gossiping, backstabbing, and bullying).

- I will not engage in the "3 B's" (Bickering, Back-biting, and Blaming). I will practice the "3 C's" (Caring, Committing, and Collaborating) in my relationship with you and ask you to do the same with me.

- I will always be open to give help, ask for help, and accept help.

- I will talk to you promptly in a private location if I am having a problem with you. The only time I will discuss it with another person is when I need advice or help in deciding how to communicate with you appropriately.

- I will remember that neither of us is perfect and that human errors are opportunities, not for shame or guilt, but for forgiveness and growth.

- I will respect and treat all coworkers equally, regardless of a person's work experience or job position.

- I will provide positive feedback to my coworkers for their quality of work and contribution to our organization.

- I will arrive and be ready to perform my job duties at my scheduled time. I will honor the time and attendance policies.

- I will put work first while on duty.

- I will be a positive example for others.

Attitude

- I will show compassion by accepting others' concerns as my own.

- I will show consideration for others by treating everyone as the most important person. Rudeness and sarcasm are never appropriate.

- I will accept constructive criticism.

- I will address problems in a professional, respectful manner.

- I will smile and make eye contact.

I am recommitting to the Behavior Standards. In particular, I have re-read the above sections on Commitment to My Coworkers and Attitude and agree to commit to being part of improving the Work Environment in our Department.

_____ Date: _____/_____/_____

Employee Signature

Leadership Learning Needs Assessment

Purpose: To assess the learning needs of our leaders in an effort to develop a leadership training/development plan.

Instructions: Please complete the assessment below utilizing the defined rating systems and also answer questions 1–6. Also, please feel free to make additional narrative comments/suggestions related to leadership training and development needs.

Please turn in your responses to _____

no later than _____.

Rating Systems:

Column 1: Skill as it relates to me succeeding in my current leadership role.

A = Critical skill — I require this skill to succeed in my role.

B = Helpful skill — This skill may help me to succeed in my role.

C = Skill not needed or rarely needed in my role.

Column 2: My current competency level of this skill.

1 = I have very little or no training/experience with this skill.

2 = I have some training/experience but need more.

3 = I've mastered this skill. I am competent to perform this skill.

Column 3: Place a checkmark on the five (5) most important leadership skills needed in order to be successful in achieving our goals.

Leadership Skills	Column 1 A, B, C	Column 2 1, 2, 3	Column 3 √
Setting and Achieving Goals			
Planning and Managing Change			
Project Management			
Time and Priority Management			
Patient Safety/Quality Improvements/ Risk Management			
Survey/Accreditation Readiness and Compliance			
Financial Management (reducing ex- penses, increasing revenues, handling billing/revenue cycle processes)			
Measuring and Improving Support Department Satisfaction			
Measuring and Improving Employee Satisfaction			
Work Flow/Process Improvement Methodologies (LEAN, etc.)			
Delegation			
Appraising/Evaluating Performance			
Creating an Effective Work Environment/Culture			
Conflict Resolution/ Difficult Conversations			
Negotiation Skills			
Satisfaction/Measurement/ Service Recovery			

Leadership Skills	Column 1 A, B, C	Column 2 1, 2, 3	Column 3 √
Rewarding and Recognizing Individuals and Groups			
Planning and Managing Growth of a Service Line			
Staffing Plans/ Productivity Management			
Team Building/Collaboration			
Data/Information (measurements/ metrics, reporting)			
Computer Skills (list specific needs in comment section)			
Financial Reports (income statement, balance sheet, ratios, etc.)			
Fostering Innovation			
Mentoring			
Philanthropy/Fundraising			
Learning Best Practices			
Public Speaking/Presentation Skills			
Marketing/Community Relations			
Hiring/Selecting Employees			
Improving Individual Performance of Employees			
Communicating More Effectively			

1. How effective is the leadership orientation program? Comments.

2. How effective are the scheduled leadership development/training programs? Comments.

3. How effective are the processes for succession planning and the development of future leaders? Comments.

4. Your years of leadership experience:

5. Level of leadership position (e.g., Senior Leader, Supervisor, Director, Lead, etc.):

6. Describe the last three leadership education/training sessions you attended (briefly describe what they were and when you attended):

Please provide any additional comments/suggestions that you feel will assist in the development of an effective leadership-training plan:

Please return to _____ **by** _____.

Thank you for your time, input, and valuable contributions to the leadership development plan.

Sample Learning Roadmap

Learning Roadmap		
	Due	*Completed Y/N*
LEAN		
Select one of the two LEAN project teams to participate in. Engage as an active member of the project team.	March 1– June 30	
Communication Plan		
With employee involvement, develop department Communication Plan.	Submit by April 1	
Rounding		
Initiate Rounding—including documentation—to be conducted each day that you work (once per week with another department/customer; the balance of the week with employee rounding).	April 1	
Follow Up, as needed, regarding Rounding (equipment needs, thank you notes, etc.).	Beginning April 1 and ongoing	
Thank You Notes		
Handwrite four Thank You Notes to be mailed to the homes of employees each month.	Beginning April 1	

Sample Employee Survey Statements

- New or transferred employees receive adequate orientation.

- My coworkers have positive attitudes.

- My coworkers are competent.

- Our department is working diligently to achieve goals.

- Our department celebrates its achievements.

- Our department delivers great customer service.

- Our department is committed to doing quality work.

- Our department welcomes new ideas.

- Our department's work flow leads to our work being done efficiently.

- Our procedures are good at preventing errors from happening.

- We have a work climate in which we can report errors.

- We openly discuss errors.

- Safety concerns are promptly addressed.

- We have a work climate that promotes error prevention.

- Our communication during shift change or handoffs is effective at preventing errors.

- I receive support from my coworkers.

- I am a member of a team that works well together.

- I have the training I need to do my job right.

- I can get answers to my questions.

- I have the equipment and supplies I need to do my job right.

- My immediate supervisor includes employees in decision-making.

- My immediate supervisor keeps me well informed.

- My immediate supervisor encourages my career growth.

- My immediate supervisor cares about me as a person.

- I receive support from my immediate supervisor.

- Leaders demonstrate good follow-through.

- Leaders have positive attitudes.

- Leaders are competent.

- Senior leaders keep employees well informed about key strategies.

- This organization makes it possible for employees to contribute to its success.

- This organization's behavior standards are adhered to by all.

- My workload is manageable.

- I am competent to do my job.

- My work expectations are clearly defined.

- My opinion matters.

- I receive weekly positive feedback for doing great work.

- My job is important to the organization's mission.

- Work stress is not interfering with my home life.

- My workload leads to exhaustion.

- My physical work space is appropriate.

- I feel empowered to do the best job I can do.

- My work is meaningful.

- I can initiate action to change things that need to be improved.

- I receive positive feedback.

- I am proud to work here.

- I like my job.

- I plan to keep working here for the next year.

- I plan to keep working here for the next five years.

- Overall, I am satisfied with my employment here.

- I recommend the services here to others.

- I recommend this place to others as a great place to work.

- Action plans developed from the last survey have had a positive impact.

Sample Employee Experience Survey Results Worksheet

What are the *organization's* ratings for the following questions:

	This Year	Last Year
I am proud to work here.	_____	_____
I would recommend this employer to a friend as a good place to work.	_____	_____
I would recommend the services here to my friends and relatives.	_____	_____
I consider myself a satisfied employee.	_____	_____

What are your *department's* ratings for the following questions:

	This Year	Last Year
I am proud to work here.	_____	_____
I would recommend this employer to a friend as a good place to work.	_____	_____
I would recommend the services here to my friends and relatives.	_____	_____
I consider myself a satisfied employee.	_____	_____

Show the results of your *department-specific employee satisfaction goal* here:

- Did you meet your goal(s) related to employee satisfaction?

- What are the three top-rated statements in your department?

- What are the three lowest-rated statements in your department?

- Any interesting observations about how your department's scores compare to other departments and/or the organization's averages?

- Which statements improved the most when compared to last year?

- Which statements decreased the most when compared to last year?

- Any interesting observations/trends in reviewing the comments?

Sample Organization-Wide and/or Department-Specific Goals

Sample 1:

Goal Statement: To increase the combined scores for four (4) key employee satisfaction survey elements by eighteen (18) or more points in one year.

Baseline: Most recent Employee Satisfaction Survey results for the four (4) statements (290.2)

Goal Measurement: Next annual Employee Satisfaction Survey results for the four (4) statements (308.2+)

Baseline/Last Year

I am proud to work here.	80.3
I would recommend this employer as a great place to work.	70.1
I consider myself a satisfied employee.	67.3
I would recommend the services here to others.	72.5
Baseline TOTAL:	290.2 (Goal: 308.2+)

Sample 2:

Goal Statement: To increase employee satisfaction on the following statements by 3 percent or more each in the next year.

Baseline: Most recent Employee Satisfaction Survey results for the following statements

Goal Measurement: Next annual Employee Satisfaction Survey results for the following statements

1. My coworkers have positive attitudes

(baseline = 68.2)

2. Our department welcomes new ideas
   (baseline = 65.3)

3. I have the training I need to do my job right
   (baseline = 69.1)

4. My immediate supervisor encourages my career growth
   (baseline = 66.6)

Sample 3:

Goal Statement: To increase the Overall Employee Satisfaction rate by 5 percent or more over last year.

Baseline: Most recent survey results for Overall Employee Satisfaction (Baseline = 76.4)

Goal Measurement: Next annual survey results for Overall Employee Satisfaction (Goal = 81.4 percent or higher)

Note: When selecting a goal for overall employee satisfaction, it may be useful to focus your action plans on two to three specific elements for improvement that are correlated to Overall Employee Satisfaction.

References

Anderson, N. R., Cunningham-Snell, N. A., & Haigh, J. 1996. "Induction training as socialization: Current practice and attitudes to evaluation in British organizations." *International Journal of Selection and Assessment*, 4, 169–183.

Ashford, S. J., & Black, J. S. 1996. "Proactivity during organizational entry: The role of desire for control." *Journal of Applied Psychology*, 81, 199–214

Lean Institute. 2014. *Lean Lexicon* (5th Edition). Lean Enterprises Institute.

Schober, P. 2013, August 14. "The Cost of a Bad Hire." Retrieved July 15, 2014.

Shah, N., Pollack, S., & Dutta, R. 2014, May 1. "Trends in workforce analytics — Capturing the latest results from US Human Capital Effectiveness Benchmarks." Retrieved August 12, 2014.

Acknowledgments

Not everybody can be famous, but everybody can be great—
because greatness is determined by service.
—Martin Luther King, Jr.

The healthcare organizations we work with may not be famous, but they are great. They perform amazing work within their communities each and every day, bringing excellence in healthcare and stellar work environments to their employees.

Without the employees, physicians, and leaders we have worked with over decades of healthcare leadership and continue to work with on a daily basis, this book would never have happened. Our gratitude is unending for the healthcare communities of:

> Sault Ste. Marie, Michigan
> Manistique, Michigan
> Platteville, Wisconsin
> Eaton Rapids, Michigan
> Richland Center, Wisconsin
> Tuba City, Arizona
> Brighton, Michigan

Some of you may recognize yourselves in our stories. Know that your impact on providing amazing leadership and improving the employee experience has impacted hundreds of leaders who have attended our Boot Camps and Summits.

Again, we thank each and every employee who works in a partner organization, has attended a training event, or has invited us in to share your employee experience with you. All of you are in our minds and hearts as we write each day. Thank you for sharing. Thank you for "just starting."

As we serve in the roles as detectives searching to uncover what makes any organization great, we have read, researched, debated, tested, and applied. The creation of the Framework, Structure, and Solutions has been inspired by the work of many forward and deep thinkers. We have read and re-read their works. Our appreciation and respect extends to many great researchers, authors, and leaders. In the acknowledgment of a sampling of these great contributors, we show our appreciation for the work of John P. Kotter, Michael H. Cohen, Quint Studer, Jim Collins, The FranklinCovey Group, Dr. Bryan Sexton, Barbara Fredrickson, and Everett M. Rogers.

Taking *The Employee Experience* Beyond the Page

About Capstone Leadership Solutions, Inc.

Capstone's vision is to inspire positive change. While Capstone serves healthcare organizations and leaders all over the country, its co-founders, Sue Tetzlaff and Jane McLeod, have a passion for rural healthcare. Sue and Jane have been healthcare clinicians and leaders for decades. They have recent experience doing what healthcare employees and leaders do. They are high energy, positive, and full of passion for their work.

Capstone is ready to serve organizations in the following ways:

- Partnership (Assessment, Planning, and Execution)

- Public Training Events: Summits, Boot Camps, and Retreats

- Customized On-Site Leadership and Employee Training

- Keynote and Conference Speaking

- Facilitation of Strategic Planning, Leadership, Board and/or Medical Staff Retreats

- Focused Improvement Projects (i.e., quality, patient satisfaction, human resources)

Capstone's monthly eNewsletter, "Just Start," is filled with best practices and resources. Sign up at: www.capstoneleadership.net.

The Scrubs to C-Suite blog provides weekly inspiration and practical advice for those making positive change. Enjoy more of Jane's and Sue's writing at: http://blog.capstoneleadership.net.

Reach Jane or Sue at:

Sue Tetzlaff
sue@capstoneleadership.net

Jane McLeod
jane@capstoneleadership.net

About Jane McLeod, co-founder, Capstone Leadership Solutions, Inc.

Working with employees to ignite the same energy and passion for their careers as she has for her own has been the cornerstone of Jane's work. She feels blessed to have been chosen to lead many new initiatives in technological advances, cost-saving measures, and improvements to the employee experience. Her work as a nursing leader has led to a tremendous increase in the satisfaction of her employees and the customers they serve. She lives under the model of Servant Leadership and walks by example every day. Jane is very proud of the fact that her career has included a variety of clinical and leadership roles, allowing her to better understand the realities and challenges facing employees and leaders.

Jane's leadership experience also included the opportunity to develop a worksite wellness program. Her passion has always included a focus on choosing a healthy lifestyle and illness prevention. She saw the results of making poor lifestyle choices while working as a nurse in an oncology and emergency room setting and has worked to show those around her that they can make simple, effective changes in their work and personal life to create dramatic changes in their health.

While very accomplished in her work endeavors, Jane feels that her greatest achievements have been her thirty-plus year marriage to her husband, Scott, and parenting her three children, who also demonstrate the same love for life that she has.

About Sue Tetzlaff, co-founder, Capstone Leadership Solutions, Inc.

Sue is known for her high expectations and never feels the need to apologize for having them. She truly believes that good is the enemy of great and that mediocrity should be, and can be, replaced with excellence. She attacks her work with energy, positivity, and passion.

As the co-founder of Capstone Leadership Solutions, she specializes in assessing organizations to facilitate planning and execution of operational improvements. Sue is passionate about helping healthcare organizations and leaders implement evidenced-based leadership and clinical practices that improve both the patient and employee experience. She has served in senior leadership positions for more than twenty years.

Improving the patient and employee experience, developing new programs, expanding services, facilitating strategic retreats, training leaders and employees, and mentoring new leaders are among the favorite aspects of her work. She has been a trainer at over sixty leadership and employee development events with the objective of training hundreds of leaders and employees on skills necessary to create extraordinary results. She has also served as a featured speaker at industry workshops and events.

In her early years, her athletic endeavors contributed to three state championship volleyball titles and a team induction into the Michigan Athletic Association's "Legends of the Game" Hall of Fame.

Sue has beautiful daughters and gentlemen for sons. She is proud of her husband, Tim, who still feels that it is a privilege to be a family practitioner after more than thirty years.